THE LORD'S REVELATION

THE ANCIENT OF DAYS AND THE SPIRIT OF JUDGEMENT

GOD'S MESSAGE TO ALL CHRISTIANS WORLDWIDE

VICTOR NYARKO AMOAH

For more information about The Lord's Revelation reach us at:

thevictorbooks@gmail.com

Other books by the author:

- THE ONE WHO WALKS AMIDST THE SEVEN GOLDEN LAMPSTANDS – VOLUME ONE

- THE ONE WHO WALKS AMIDST THE SEVEN GOLDEN LAMPSTANDS – VOLUME TWO

- THE SEVENTH HORN OF THE LAMB OF GOD'S SPOKEN MYSTERY OF CHRIST'S BODY AND BLOOD – THE VICTORS' WEAPON IN TRIBULATIONS

- THE APPEALING VOICE OF THE SENTRY ANGEL "FEAR NOT I'M WITH HIM"

- THE MYSTERY OF THE MOUNT OF CONGREGATION FROM THE HIGH PRIEST MELCHIZEDEK

- THE SIXTH HORN OF THE LAMB OF GOD AND THE WARFARE OF THE ABOMINATION OF DESOLATION

- THE OTHER COMFORTER-THE LIVING WITNESS ON EARTH AND IN HEAVEN

- THE TRILOGY OF WITNESSES: THE COMFORTER, THE SPIRIT OF GRACE AND SUPPLICATION AND GOD'S WISDOM

Copyright © 2020

ISBN: 9798332410444

ALL RIGHTS RESERVED

AUTHOR'S NOTE

PREFACE

THE ANCIENT OF DAYS.

CHAPTER 1.

CHAPTER 2.

CHAPTER 3

CHAPTER 4

CHAPTER 5

CHAPTER 6.

GOD'S SPIRIT OF JUDGEMENT.

CHAPTER 1.

CHAPTER 2.

CHAPTER 3

AUTHOR'S NOTE

Readers are advised to acknowledge that this book contains a lot of mysteries that require divine enlightenment for true comprehension. For this reason, it should not be read without scriptural accompaniment. In effect the Bible must always be available when reading this book; prayers and fasting should also be utilized.

To reiterate: Do not ever read this book without the Bible. The Bible confirms all aspects of the Revelation, so if you read and you do not understand, take a deep breath, say a prayer, then read it over again and the Lord will provide a more perfect, divine comprehension.

We encourage everyone to endeavor to avail themselves of this book which is designed to help them as they strive to find total perfection in the Lord.

May the Lord be with all obedient servants of the Lamb's new Israel. Amen!

PREFACE

This is the voice of the total perfection of God, speaking in the Ancient of Days. He is the beginning and the end, and the preparer of the path of righteousness. God, the Ancient of Days has projected His perfection and is admonishing all humans to critically examine their modes of worship. God does not want to encounter any nuisances on the day of His entry into the sanctuary. For God will project His Spirit of vengeance at the close of all creation in order to prove all modes of worship as to whether they conform to the order and will of heaven.

Human beings apply their physical elements such as the lips, tongues, hands and others, as well as their conscience elements being the mind, the heart, the conscience, realization and understanding in their worship of God. All these elements require a certain level of sanctity spiritually, as a prerequisite for all worships to please God. Faith is the power by which all these are bound into one in the will of God, for the worship of God to draw men into the required level of glory as in Christ. This is the reason, the sacrifices of the elements that commit abomination are abhorrent to God and the prayers of deceitful tongues are also an abomination to Him.

The power of faith resides in the ability of the spiritual elements' total affirmation on righteousness, in order be not built on that which is seen with the eyes. For a believer to tread in absolute firmness, he must build his faith on divine powers and not on physical things seen by the eyes. The faith of Christ's disciples suffered a lot of persecution because it was built on the person of Christ. Satan was therefore much alert to scatter them on the day Christ would be taken to heaven. He did the very same, having gotten Stephen murdered and scar the disciples into flight.

When Christ however got his hands on Saul, He seized him to lead the ministry he had persecuted; even unto the time he was taken into the third heavens. He was meticulously tutored by the Ancient of Days about the carefulness required of prophets and priests in the ministry of faith. Satan became extremely jealous about Paul in the faith and for that matter tempted him on countless occasions to apply his own mind in addition to the teachings of the divine gospel. Very truly, the faith that leads into eternal life is the one that possesses the will of God and not the one which owns the name of God. For this reason, no matter any difficulties, the believer must possess the will of God, just in the manner in which Christ submitted to the will of His Father; for it is the will of God that absolves one from judgement. **John 5:27.**

God's spirit of Judgement is ever alert against all who worship, without possessing the will of God because God projected the truth of His accomplished will through His Son Jesus Christ. God, through His Son abrogated the first covenant and established the second one, and ordained Him in charge as a High Priest. Stringent judgement awaits all who teach people the worship of God but have departed from God's will which He projected through His Son, and their followers because they failed to remain alert and have trusted in deceit. They are like the first Adam to believe in deceit and have therefore demonstrated themselves as an adversary of the second Adam.

The dragon has fashioned the deceit which came from the serpent into a life-giving trust for the believers seized into the serpent's deceit. God's name has therefore chained them into perdition, for they have not received the enlightening realization of the second Adam. This separation is actively firm between the children of the Lamb and the offspring of the serpent; being unknown to the serpent that it is an affirmed promise of perdition. They persecute the children of the Lamb for they take for themselves an enemy, the healing power that the stripes of Christ provide. The descendants of the second Adam, bought with the blood of the Lamb are awaiting the glory of the precious faith and have therefore separated themselves from judgement by being alert. The Ancient of Days, being the Alpha and Omega and God's Spirit of Judgement have revealed these mysteries, to beckon all Christians worldwide, who by faith have prepared themselves to be absolved from judgment.

THE ANCIENT OF DAYS.

CHAPTER 1.

The Ancient of Days is in His Temple and will avenge those who by their actions desecrate it.

1. I am Alpha and Omega, the beginning and the end. It is imperative that I speak to you, son of the earth, for you to understand that, I opened your spiritual ears so that you will be able to hear spiritual things. I started with you and it is I, who will end with you. I am the Ancient of Days; one whose days and time never end. I exist for ever and ever. **Revelation 20:11-12.** The way I lived with your forebearers, so do I lead you of today as well. **Isaiah 41:4-5.** Who can ever stop or alter what I Jehovah God have planned? I am speaking to you

again for the reason that, all nations have gone astray but they employ my name Jehovah in the search of earthly wealth. I want you people, to be very careful about this phenomenon.

2. My anger is raging against those who mention the name Jehovah, because they employ my name to conjure false powers and that's baffling too many people on earth. But as for you, if you obey these words and demonstrate a change of mind, my anger will abate and will have mercy on those who will receive these messages without doubt. I revealed to the earlier prophets and they are my witnesses that is it by divine counsel that I always deliver people from destruction. The prophet Isaiah saw my glory with his eyes. **Isaiah 6:1-7.** He ought not to have seen me but after he did, he immediately confessed the sins of his lips It was these acts of Isaiah that saved him from death. So do I Jehovah do till today. One who proves his steps

and does confessions will have my salvation by all means. **Psalms 50:22-23.**

3. I know humans do not appreciate the fullness of my Godhead. The way humans ought to acknowledge me as their creator and call upon me to deliver them in times of troubles is unknown to them. I have therefore imbued the nature of man to recognize me in cultural allusions to Alpha and Omega, which pronouncement the lip does with ease. Alpha and Omega therefore take the short form of AO on the lips of many when found in troubles or in the threats of fear. Humans in their inability to be alert with prompt invocation of the name of God in their difficulties have the natural endowment of unconscious reference to the name of God, so they would be saved by his power unawares. I am revealing this to you as a proof that I Jehovah God, am the beginning and the end.

Many pronounce this name howbeit, without true realization.

4. One who will invoke the name Jehovah with faith and realization will receive a prompter response than one who does so without faith and realization. Jehovah God will deliver all who call upon His name, just as it has been written. **Romans 10:13-16.** This scripture indicates that, there is the need to send the proclaimers of the gospel to the nation of God. I cite my servant, prophet Isaiah as an example in this case. His testimonies are a confirmation that, believing in the scriptures evoke the fear of the Lord. In spite of all the testimonies of Isaiah as indicated, completely different things are being done in these last days. The invokers of the name of God are over abundant but believers in Him are scarce. Take care therefore not to remain believers in proclamations by lips but rather steadfast believers. I will continue to speak to you,

therefore, to get you awake out of your ignorance. **Isaiah 48:1-9.**

5. Satan and his army are in fierce rage against you for being used as a vessel to proclaim my messages, the reason for which they have conceived a firm plan to set a trap for you, Victor, to get you out of the land of the living. You therefore ought to be particularly alert, including your whole household, from the children up to the grown-ups. Look! Once the Lord continues to speak to you, be aware that the accuser of your kind is standing at your doors. The whole church ought to be very much alert. Do not let your heart tremble about what I am revealing to you about your adversary and do not be shaken by fear. The same manner in which I covered the earlier prophets with my hands, so do I remain forever and would execute whatever I have planned with nothing

stopping me. I am the Amen. **Isaiah 49:6-10.** I speak and it must manifest.

6. You son of the earth, do not fear your enemies. Hold fast to fervent prayers and make sure your Amen proclamation is sound because I am the Amen. When you are in supplication and pronounce the name of the source of authority, what then can prevent the manifestation of your request on its time? The devil causes people to doze during prayer sessions and they are therefore not awake to the proclamation of the Amen for the prayers. I am the Amen in the midst of the church, therefore learn the proclamation of Amen. **Revelation 3:14-16.** Dozing during prayer sessions renders the prayer lukewarm and imperfect. People who doze and those who keep their minds off the prayers should know that they cause the prayer to be weak. The Amen proceeds from the Father, working through the Son, providing the

proclaimers with that power. **2 Corinthians 1:20-22.**

7. It should be clear to prayer subjects that, a disorderly proclamation of Amen disrupts the prayer. Therefore, examine what the scripture says carefully. It is the promises of God that ought to be mentioned in the prayers and when the promises come clearly, then the Amen is conducted by the promised words into the Lord and projects through the power of the Lord into the Son and returns to the proclaimer, thus drawing the praise power of God to the prayer subject. If the supplicant does not apply the promises of God but rather engages in talkativeness and repetitions, the prayer gets prolonged uselessly. A prayer that ends in talkativeness is a mere waste of time. Look! I declare to you that, if the prayers consist of the words of the promise, the Amen proceeds from the ransom fruit of the Lord to seal the prayers and

thus provoking timely response. If the prayer is under the command of the Holy Spirit, the ransom of the spirit inherent in it causes the audience to realize the need to pronounce the Amen.

8. It is imperative to proclaim Amen in all prayers the reason for which the audience must understand the words of the prayers clearly to ensure that the mind and faith are attuned to it for the Amen to be proclaimed. One ought not proclaim Amen on that which is not understood. **1 Corinthians 15:17.** Learn the proper prayer practice. The messages of prophet Isaiah confirm that the lips of I, Jehovah have provided words in sufficient abundance to offer light and knowledge to all nations. In these last days however, it is rather places where my name is proclaimed that vices are abundant. These actions have rendered the house of the Lord an abode of robbers. People are employing the name of I, the lord in thievery

and robbery and my name is used to seduce their colleagues, spouses in these days. It is those who by vicious schemes search for gains that serve in these days as priests and prophets. **Isaiah 33:13-17.** Temples are filled with adultery while their ladies hurry in twisting their waists thus desecrating my sanctuary. I lament that, 'AO' my sanctuary has been turned into an awful horror. This is the outcome of the behaviours of the patrons who worship in it. Yes! It is their vices. They draw vices into their prayers. **Isaiah 42:18-21.**

9. I am speaking to you about all things that corrupt the temple. The underlying factors causing the desecration of the temple is the removal of the statutes of I, Jehovah from their places of worship and the instituting of orders meant to obtain money, wealth and the comforts of the world. They set aside the commandments of I, Jehovah, their creator and their maker. Be alert with fervent

prayers so that when you hear these messages, you don't throw them behind you but rather commit them into memory and practice them.

10. I am that I am. I am reminding you again that, due to these messages that I reveal to you, the enemy has a firm plan to wage war against you to prevent you from writing. But I command you to continue writing without fear. **Isaiah 5:12-16.** These are the things that I notice, for which I speak to you. The first issue concerns the quality of all your chapels. This poses the need that I speak to you by all means so that you will remain alert. Your chapel was not built with financial support sought from robbers and the hands of murderers and accused people have not been found to have contributed anything. No support was sought from the great men of this world or from any spirit for the construction. No special powers were buried in the ground before the construction. No spiritual

debts have been incurred, in the construction of the chapel for which patrons should be used for the settlement of any spiritual restitutions. Understand it also that, the size of the chapel, be it large or small has nothing to do with its being a chapel, but rather it is the things that I have enumerated to you earlier that are causes of desecration to the chapel.

11. If you will be alert and will not permit any of these desecrating factors to get into your midst in your chapels, then I can dwell among you with courage and I will let your chapels remain life invigorating ones. Dot not ever leave your altars in the control of women and never leave them to the service of any state authority. Never invite any special persons to the altar so that you do not use the need for chapel building money and pledges as a means of committing the chapel into the abode of bulls and dogs as a result of what they offer you.

Remember my commandments and statutes, for I am your Lord, God, I do not change. Do not ever send a dead body into your chapel, so that you will not desecrate it. I want you to hold fast to all that I am telling you, therefore, write them down for the alertness of all generations. **Isaiah 48:20-22.** Separate yourselves from all that desecrate you and your chapels. It is very important.

12. The order of the day is that, the enemy has robbed them all, of the spirit of discernment and the proof of things, for which reason they accept all concepts into their mode of worship provided it will offer some worldly benefits. They never think about whether it pleases God or not. As for me, I remain who I am. I declare myself with this name as a proof that I never change forever and ever. **Hebrews 13:7-10.** It is to be noted that the orders of the temple and the altar must never be changed. The purpose of the Revelation which you are

receiving presently is that, you should notice how your forebears fellowshipped with I, Jehovah, so that you the latter generations will use their weaknesses as examples to redeem your ways. When you as well read how some of your forebears also remained faithful to the pleasure of God, you will learn of their righteousness and mend your ways as well. It is for the reason of you not desecrating your chapel and also not drawing your altar into sacrilege that I am issuing these instructions of remembrance. Some people laid the temple's foundations, but during the construction the devil attempted to draw sacrilege into the project.

13.   When the project initiators realized that sacrilege was tempting, they immediately rejected the support of their agents. **Ezra 4:1-5.** You will observe from this scripture that since the initiators realized by their wakefulness and rejected the help

of the sacrilegious group, the enemy incited this group to weaken the bands of the builders with laziness and to threaten them to not continue with the project. At that very hour, the eyes of I, the Ancient of Days saw what was going on and knew it came from the devil. Since I was not pleased with their attempts, I quickly responded to the initiators' prayer from my glorious abode when they called me; I therefore gave them full support to build the temple to its perfect state. **Haggai 1:14-15.** I want you to understand this clearly that, the way the enemy waged war against the building of the temple in the days of old, so is he still at war with those who are building their spiritual temples for eternal life today.

14. It is recorded in the scripture that God does not dwell in buildings made by hand. **Acts. 17:24.** This message is thus clear that I queried that a temple be built for me, so I could dwell in the midst

of my nation, and I ordered in those days that the temple should be built for my name. I would have severely chastised my nation if they had refused to put up the building. **Haggai 1:1-11.** How would I, who queried and punished the inhabitants of the earth for not putting up a place for me, say then that I do not dwell in buildings made with hand? My dwelling in a hand-built temple or otherwise stems from the behaviour of those who patronize and worship in it. It is because of their sacrilegious behaviours that I am unable to dwell among them. When King David attempted to build a temple for Jehovah God in the days of old, he procured everything ready for the construction. While the king was not alert, the devil led him to kill a woman's husband stealthily and took the woman as his wife. This action was so vicious, for which he did not deserve to build a temple for Jehovah with blood-stained hands. David became very remorseful after I rejected his building offer, and therefore made a prayer of repentance. **Psalms 51:1-21.**

15. The King repented but had no chance to put up the building. When his son Solomon, whose hands were not blood-stained as his father's offered to build me a temple, did I tell him that I do not dwell in buildings made by the hands, so if he completed it should he not invite me into it? Look! Let me tell you; I am the Beginning and the End and I never change. If the temple has no sacrilegious marks, I am compelled to recall what I declared to Solomon and let them be manifest for you about the chapel. **2 Chronicles 7:11-16.** Once I promised the forebears that all these things will be fulfilled for them, I ought to do the very same for the later generation as well. All these are coming forth for your recollection and alertness so that you will remove all sacrilegious things from amongst you so that your chapels will enjoy the grace of the Lord. I

am not Jehovah in the era of Solomon alone. Look! I am Jehovah and I am forever through all generations.

16. Your priests ought to pray fervently, so that they do not in any way serve as conduit for sacrilege onto your altars. Satan rose against Israel and deceived King David in many instances. **I Chronicles 21:1-3.** The way Satan deceived King David and the whole nation of Israel, so is he out deceiving priests and churches today, that they apply blasphemy to defile the sanctuary. Look! Be very much alert. It is written, my house shall be called a temple and nothing else. It is the things that I revealed to the earlier prophets that I continue to reveal to you priests of today, that there is no way you people would force any orders on God. Those things observed by the earlier prophets as sacrilegious are the very things the children of today adopt as steps of enlightenment.

If you could be privileged to interview any of the olden day priests about the things being done in the temples of today, you would find out clearly that, it is their quality of life that is exposing the wrongs of the priests and prophets of today. **Haggai 2:8-19.**

17. This scripture indicates that, the nation or the church ought to question their leaders for it is their responsibility to teach them how to hold themselves holy so they don't render the sanctuary into sacrilege. It is a reality that God does not dwell in building made by the hand. This being the case, does it also follow that, the human beings in whom Jehovah is a living spirit also do not dwell in buildings constructed by the hands of humans? They dwell in them, the reason for which it is clear that it is the behaviour of the patrons of the temples that cause God not to dwell in the temples constructed by the hands of men. The way some of

the earlier people daubed themselves with idols before coming to kneel down in the sanctuary, so is the enemy using humans today to desecrate the sanctuary. **Ezekiel 8:3-6.**

18. This scripture affirms, the elders of Israel, who worship on the altar of Jehovah are the same people who practice the culture of desecration, so it is in these days of ours. If any of the olden day priests should be questioned as to whether it is proper for someone to touch a corpse before coming to the tent of God, they know it very well that it is a sacrilege. Do the priests of today also not know it? **Haggai 2:13-15.** Understand it that, from the very beginning, if anybody set his mind up to establish an abode for the Lord, the enemy started a war, even before the person laid the first foundation stone. The enemy watches the construction from the onset and attempts to incite the hearts of the builders with sacrilege so that

their actions would prevent God from dwelling in the sanctuary. Pray to God to know your needs and provide them for you in your requests. I Jehovah do not want humans to perish; that is why I continue to speak.

19. It should be clear to you that a human being can consume what is abhorrent to him provided he so wishes but Jehovah God can never tolerate what is abhorrent to Him. Amend your ways with these messages for the time is due for all temples to be demolished without leaving a stone unturned. **Luke 21:5-8.** That which caused the destruction of the temple was that, the patrons did not consider the fact that the one in whose name it was built is holy, so the patrons who call upon his name should as well as be holy. If your physical temples endeavour to teach righteousness and draws people away from sacrilege, your inner spiritual temples will not be demolished. People who really worship me are

those whose spiritual temples are upright. If the behaviour of the patrons of the physical chapel do not conform to the exact order of the Lord, it causes imperfection in their spiritual chapels. They shall be demolished for their lack of perfection.

20. If you put up chapels with marbles and their patrons are sacrilegious, it means they are only baffling themselves with outward nature and their spiritual chapels are uncompleted. Fight hard to make sure your spiritual temples are not demolished, but rather grow in the love of the Holy Spirit to become strongly established temples for the Lord **1 Corinthians 6:19-20.**

It is written, nothing defiles except for the person who considers something as defiling. **Romans 14:14.** This is a commandment regarding the lifestyles of humans. The scripture expresses further that, it defiles only for the person who considers it so. The understanding of this scripture has become burdensome to you, the reason for which many people no longer think of things that are sacrilegious to God. I declare to you that I am Jehovah, it is my name.

21.   That which someone considers sacrilegious cannot be changed to his acceptance by another person. In the same way, no power can change the stand of I, Jehovah, about the things that I have mentioned to be sacrilegious to me and I will accept them. Powers from within the spirit of I, Jehovah have already told you a lot of things. If I however continue to speak to you, you should learn it that it is not so much the issues of the flesh that I am referring to, but matters of the spirit. I have perfect trust that if you continue to read the words of the spirits which have already spoken to you and hold fast to their instructions, you will realize all spiritual sacrileges. For instance, the commandment of holiness which requires that

hands and fact should be washed before entering the sanctuary is a mere outward action which has nothing to do with soul and spirit. What is required to be known regarding the spirit is to learn spiritual holiness. **James 4:7-12.**

22. It is written, one person is the author of the commandment and He again is the Judge. If someone washes hands and feet but remains a verbal assailant and is quarrelsome, I declare that no chapel belonging to a quarrelsome person shall stand. Look! If the priests of today were alert in what I said through my servant Isaiah, it would have been very difficult for them to be led astray. And now, they have changed the chapel and the altar to a place for the search of worldly wealth and many altars have become places of magical enchantment – woe unto them. **Isaiah 3:7-13.** I Jehovah, will make manifest that which I have made to be written down, each according to its

time. You ought to change your minds when you read my instructions, so that none of you will tempt the Lord. I am reminding you once again that, that which I am known to be from the beginning, is that which remain. If you children of today however lack the understanding of my words, then read about the people of the olden days, who walked with me, so that you will know who, I, Jehovah am. **Isaiah 22:12-14.**

23. Enquire from the ancient people what happened when Phinehas killed the man and the woman? If the sons of Eli, the priest defiled women in the presence of the Lord and perished, will the children of today commit such abhorrent vices and remain alive? **Isaiah 42:5-9.** It is I, Jehovah who prophesy and it is fulfilled. The nation which refuses to revere me pours sufferings on itself. The fashion of today is for all to learn to mention the name of the Lord and since they are able to

mention my name, they believe they are worshipping Jehovah God. Look! The mere mention of Jehovah does not guarantee the possession of His perfect worship order. They mention Jehovah repeatedly but their worship order is at variance with my precepts. That which they did, for which the Son did not find pleasing with them in that generation are the very things those who call upon the Lord today are doing. This is the reason the Son called them a twisted, adulterous generation; for they call the Son their Lord but refuse to comply with His teachings. **Luke 6:46.**

24. They mention Jehovah incessantly but never think of searching after His orders, let alone turn their worship orders thereunto. I confirm to you once again that, I don't change. It is you humans, who change for the worse. **Hebrews 13:8-9.** If anyone should ask you, why is Jehovah God still speaking to humans today, answer him that, it is

because they build numerous temples for the name of God but never ask about His orders in them. I promised my servant Solomon that, I will ensure that the honour of my name will be found in the temple that he will build. **2 Chronicles 7:11-16.** Behold! The pronouncements I made on Solomon's temple during his day will forever remain throughout all generations.

25. Remember that, heaven and earth shall pass away but my words shall never pass away. When I declared to Adam alone in the garden of Eden that, he will suffer and thorns and briers shall grow against him and that, dust was he and unto it shall be return, those curses did not manifest on him, who alone heard them with his ears; latter generations might not have been affected by these curses. Let it be known to you that, it is to one person only that God speaks, for compliance by all generations. It was only one woman I told in the

Garden of Eden that, she will suffer in conception, will labour before delivery and her mind will be on the husband. If this were a declaration unto Eve alone, it would not have been manifesting on all women. Was it not unto a single couple that I declared be fruitful and multiply and subdue the earth? And now their descendants are multiplying up till today, for the reason that, all that proceeds from the mouth of the Lord must accomplish its tasks before returning to me. **Isaiah 55:10-13.**

26. It was to Abraham alone I gave the covenant of circumcision, but it got manifest for all his descendants. And now, I, Jehovah God have risen to see whether my orders prescribed for Solomon's temple are being observed in the temples of today. It was revealed to prophet Isaiah that the manifestation of the prophecies of the temple shall be the honour and glory of the Lord and it shall remain an everlasting souvenir. I take you for a

witness, dear reader that: Are my orders prescribed for Solomon's temple having perfect fulfillment in the temples of today? Watch the temples critically, you who are reading this, and you will know the response to give. Should God not want to know the reason why His orders for the temples are not getting manifest? It is not that God has refuted the manifestation of His orders for the temples but rather, it is the actions of the patrons who enter and exit that prevent God and have rendered the temples a mockery in the eyes of the secular world. **Zephaniah 1:1-7.**

27. My intention was revealed to prophet Zephaniah so that their descendants would read and remain alert so that they do not become members of the group of the condemned. The Lord is out and His spirit of vengeance is wandering because the time of His spirit of grace is running out, to be replaced by vengeance. **Psalms 94:1-7.** It

is the exact nature of what is taking place in the sanctuary that has been described in the Psalm. In place of the manifestation of God's blessing to those who proclaim His name, vengeance rather shall befall them, for their temples having been filled with vices. If my spirit finds no fault with a temple and its worship order, its patrons should be alert to not fall into temptation.

28. I declared that I will eliminate idolatry from the face of the earth and I will go ahead and exterminate all who proclaim God but repose their trust in inordinate powers. I will go on and destroy all who bow to Jehovah but their powers are concealed in odd heavenly sources. I will make sure I destroy all who bow to the Lord but their worship orders are at variance with the Lord's. I will ensure I annihilate all those who claim Jehovah as their God but have adulterated their worship orders with vicious doctrines. They shall all perish for

proclaiming the name of Jehovah without adhering to his commandments and orders. **Zephaniah 1:1-6.** The wise amongst you should change their lifestyles. All that I Jehovah seek of humans is repentance and that people should have a change of mind and seek after the Lord their God. Look, you, don't cause God's spirit of vengeance to befall you. An obedient nation which takes advice and turns from its evil ways will have God's grace. **Zephaniah 3:1-5.**

29. God seeks His commandments in all His sanctuaries. False doctrines are evil in the eyes of I, Jehovah. If humans should endeavour to give my name to ulterior creations or apply my name in complying with false doctrines and vicious orders; making false claims that it is Jehovah who said it, I Jehovah will revenge against them for having blemished my name. I am God, The Ancient of Days. The reason I released my spirit of revenge

through Moses to cause an Israelite kill his Israelite neighbour was that, they likened me to a golden calf and the foolish priest taught the nation to say that the golden calf was Jehovah. This was how destruction raided them in the wilderness. **Exodus 32:3-11.** I emphasize it to you once again that I, do not change. What seriously angered me against the priest Aaron is how he mentioned Jehovah for a golden calf. This made the nation to not use the least reason against the calf since they had total trust in him as a priest. He thus told a lie that, the calf which has no life in it, let alone possess any power was that on which the priest pronounced blessing and called the God of the nation. **Exodus 32:3-6.**

30. I emphasize to you that, it is not after gold alone that the temples of today are longing but silver as well; having turned the temples unto the search for the good things of the world, neglecting

the salvation of their souls. Even though Moses prayed when I got angered and wanted to destroy the nation, I had already released my spirit of revenge onto the nation, and when it fell on Moses, he ordered that each and every one should kill his neighbour. It was this same Moses who had pleaded with God to not destroy the nation. The descent of my spirit of revenge on Moses caused, he, who prayed and pleaded that the nation should not die, used the same lips with which he pleaded to give the order that "kill your neighbours". Look! Who will not fear the living God? **Exodus 32:25-29.** I caused what pleased the nation to befall it because they mentioned my name unto a golden calf. Look! Notice this fact that when God's spirit of revenge is released, grace ceases to work.

31. I am sounding these into your ears; you who proclaim God and bow before Him, that, amend your doctrines and worship orders and turn unto

the Lord so that you will find favour with Him. Recall into mind, all you, who pray in the name of Jesus that, if I release my spirit of vengeance on the Son, this very Jesus will give orders that, those who pray in His name and still hold onto vicious behaviour should be killed – this Jesus who died the death of atonement for men. His name in heaven is the Word of God. **Revelation 14:17-20.** If you had understood the message of the revelation, you would understand the actions of God's spirit of vengeance so you will fear God. The revelation said that, the angel came from the temple in heaven, wielding a sickle. What did he go into the temple with the sickle to do? Look! This is the indication that the patrons of the temple are so corrupt that, all that they are good for is a sickle.

32. The Son drew a whip against people as a result of the vices they committed in the temple during their time. It was for people to repent from their

wrong doings that the Son drew the whip to serve as a warning. In spite of this, humans continue to do worse things even in these days. Children of today rob each other in the guise of serving God. They defile their neighbour's spouses in the name of God. The gathering of their youth in the house of God offers them the opportunity for sexual intimacy. When they gather in the presence of God during festivals, it becomes a chance to engage in illicit friendship. Will God remain silent for one to kill his neighbour by spells and take his place as a priest? Look! Great is the number of those who tread the path of vices, who still proclaim God as if they were righteous. Now then, it is no longer a whip that will be wielded by God's spirit of vengeance, but rather, a sharp sickle.

33. If you will clearly understand the revelation, you will know that the grape vine represents the vicious deeds of the inhabitants of the earth. How

could a squeezed vine be turned into blood instead of wine? This represents the multitude of the patrons of the chapels, who shall endure the vengeance of God. **Revelation 14:20.**

34. When you hear all these warnings, it behooves you to repent and make serious efforts to turn unto the life-giving precepts. **Micah 1:2-3.** Prophet Micah is giving confirmation that the time is up for God to stroll and demand accountability from chapels and their patrons. What is rather surprising is that, the more God waits to see if a time will come when they would turn unto the life-giving precepts, the more they introduce worse and filthier things into practice. A witch could kill with witchcraft but could have the guts to defend the act with God and His temple. When a sorcerer and a charmer commit murder, they give excuses with God and His temple, so as to escape judgement and revenge – woe unto them. I am explaining these for

you to know that, evil men cannot persist in evil and expect to have refuge with God. Pray that such evil men do not make your chapels and gathering places a spiritual den for robbers and foxes. The chapels and the gathering places of saints shall be called the house of God.

35. Take care therefore, that patrons of the chapel do not corrupt it with their vices, so as to render it a den for robbers. **Matthew 21:12-13.** Truly, do I declare to you that if the temple and its worship order do not conform to the rules of the worship of God, the temple draws God's anger unto itself. All that I am telling you are happening spiritually, but those on whom God finds no fault and their temples shall be blessed. Endeavour to choose the life-giving order so that God will bless your temples in exceeding measure. **Zephaniah 2:1-3.** These Revelation shall guide your steps if you use them

properly, so your worship will not become filthy when you gather in the presence of God.

36. Many people seem to consider God to be too far away in these end times. The fact remains that, God is close to those who call on Him in the spirit of truth. Look! In what spirit will someone be, to call I, Jehovah, to answer him instantly? I declare that observe my commandments and precepts and live long. **Leviticus 18:1-5.** The precept that gives life proceeds from me and it is from me that the precept that does not give life proceed. **Ezekiel 20:24-25.** After I led the nation out of bondage, I knew they were going to share boundaries with other nations. I also know that the enemy would beguile them to follow after the orders and traditions of other nations. This is the reason I gave them my life-giving precepts immediately. The nation tried to adhere to the orders, but they strayed completely after a brief period. **Ezekiel**

20:10-13. My anger got enraged against them in the wilderness thereafter.

37. Look! I am the same today and my anger is on fire even presently. How dare those who call on me pick half of my orders and mix them with half of the orders of the nations and name it as the worship orders of I, Jehovah God? I abhor all Samaritan cultures. **2 Kings 17:35-41.** Turn unto the life-giving precepts so that I Jehovah will also turn to you completely. I am explaining all these to you, to understand that, when God speaks to one person, He means a whole nation. This must be known to you humans. I spoke with Jacob as a single man, but any person who will comply with the commandments and orders I gave him, he shall have the blessings of my covenant. I shall by all means, make manifest my blessings for the one who conforms and adheres to my orders, for it is written down. **Isaiah 56:1-8.** Look! Just as my

words followed Jacob, so will it exactly manifest for the generation which pays attention to my covenant and adhere to it.

38. I testify to you about my house, that God's house shall be called a temple. **Isaiah 56:6-8.** It is written that, "my house shall be the temple for all nations". Why then do they not comply with my commandments and orders in their chapels? Many priests have been imbued with the excessive love for money and the search for worldly treasure, and have, with these, desecrated their daily sacrifices, and thus rendered their altars lifeless. The multitudes who patronize their chapels are unable to receive the seal of the power of the truth. They are replete with the vicious desires of the awful horror. That which has been written through prophet Hosea has therefore manifested on them. **Hosea 4:12-14.** As it has be written that: "I will not punish them for their fornication and adultery", so

is it getting fulfilled today. It however should be made known to you that, none of these vicious people will have God's favour. If I do not revenge today, it does not mean I will never ever avenge these desecrated folks. Look! If my time of revenge is due, I will throw my spirit of vengeance on the temples and I will avenge for their vicious lifestyles.

39. That which is vile and is equal to idolatry in the eyes of God is to ascribed to a different worship and attribute God's name to it. There is no atonement for such a vicious act. For what reason do they conceal the real power performing the miracles among them and rather proclaim Jehovah with all enthusiasm? Those who do these and all who patronize their waywardness are the very embodiment of their own actions. God will judge His nation, and woe betides those who will fall into this judgement. **Hebrews 10:30-31.** Look! My vengeance will not be hastened on those who

defile themselves with the actions of the awful horror and also come to kneel in my chapel. My seeming quietude make them think there is no revenge. The reason I warned about the entry of the awful horror into the sanctuary is for people to be alert and watch against the day it will attempt to enter, so that they will not allow themselves to be possessed. The question poses itself; how many of these chapels and their patrons are alert to watching and fleeing from it? **Matthew 24:15-16.**

Chapter 2.

The prayers of abominable tongues and lips are abhorrent to God but the selection of the holy family resides in righteous marriage.

1. The warning of this scripture, that people should run unto mountain means that people should discard all iniquity. Look! I am Jehovah Almighty. Anybody, who thinks within himself that I ever change is sure to deceive himself. I am the Ancient of Days and I don't change. I commanded Moses to ensure that the children of Israel comply with my commandments and orders. If perchance the present-day Israel are unable to comply with my commandments and precepts that does not in any

instance weaken my might. Look! I have enough courage reposed in the spiritual Israelites that they will flee from the spirit of corruption, if they hear my instructions and repent. This vicious spirit is called "the man of sin". Be alert so that you do not get defiled by this man of sin. I, Jehovah gave these commandments. **Deuteronomy 22:5.** If humans in their liberal advancement stray away from realizing what I Jehovah consider as abomination and flout my orders, that does not occasion any change in I, Jehovah God.

2. Is it not in these that most of the patrons of today's chapels are immersed, claiming they are civilized? The man of sin has opened their eyes into corruption and their liberal advancement has rendered them captives to evil deeds until their final destruction beyond any rehabilitation. I commanded that "man should remain holy, for I am holy". **Hebrews 12:14. I Peter 1:13-16.** If I

decree that something is evil, a desecration or unholy, it does not apply only to the era in which I made the declaration but it applies to people in all generations. I commanded that, no one should render himself unholy or defile himself. I am Jehovah God". **Leviticus 15:16-19.** How come that a lady who applies her tongue and lips in songs of praise to I Jehovah would desire to play with a young man's phallus in her mouth, suck and enjoy his cum and come back with that defiled tongue to the presence of God in His sanctuary?

3. Any woman, who indulges in this defiles herself and even a beast deserves more respect from God than such a one – beast they are. **Proverbs 14:32-35.** God is angered against them by all means. If a man applies his tongue and lips in prayer to God, but could apply the same tongue and lips to offer carnal pleasure to a lady in between her thighs, then such lips can no longer call God to respond

because they have been defiled and have become real abomination. If the sons of this generation can defile themselves by the use of their tongues and lips on the womanhood of women, how can I Jehovah God respond to the prayers of such lips? Look, Just as I lived with the earlier generation, so do I remain with the latter generation.

4. I let myself to be seen by the prophet Isaiah, and my spirit of vengeance declared him guilty instantly because his lips were unholy. **Isaiah 6:1-7.** If Isaiah had not cried out to me and sought deliverance, he would have perished, just for the unholiness of his lips If the lips of the earlier people were atoned for, then there must be atonement today as well through the cup of the covenant blood of the Son. Be awake and aware that, the villain knows that, it is the scripture that is leading people through the righteous pathway, so it has also planned to use the sections of the scripture which people do not

understand properly to trap them into a fall. Recall that when the tempter came to tempt Jesus, it was he who first alluded to the scripture. The devil most of the times uses the proverbs in the scripture to deceive people. For instance, if in the words of Proverbs 5:15-19, a fool can refer to the sexual organ of a woman as a well, the truth of God's blessing cannot be restricted into the things of a woman. If people do not understand this proverb, none should, out of stupidity defile himself. What would be thought of a mother, who opens her thighs for her child who comes to her to ask for water?

5. Any nursing mother who observes her child's hunger breastfeeds it. It would be a nuisance to a mother whose child grows up and would like to continue suckling on her, even though there is no nature's law against it. I am advising any man, who wants to have something doing with his tongue on

a woman to rather suck her breasts because that is what he has learnt from childhood; but should keep in him that he has outgrown breastfeeding. None of you should consider these as more instructions and refuse to abide by them, for anyone who would go against these rules will not be forgiven. **Proverbs 11:30-31.** Who knows the lifestyles of the people in Isaiah's era? Isaiah himself did not know that certain lifestyles made his lips unholy, so he got frightened when he met the glory of the Lord's light. You therefore ought to take note of the body's element called the tongue, so you will learn how to use your tongue and lips with care. **James 3:6.** Your tongues will lead you into unrighteousness if you let them loose in freedom.

6. This is how the devil has been fighting with people from the very beginning, but those who obey the instructions of I, Jehovah God are always

delivered from his deception. Just as I spoke with the ancient people, so do I continue to speak today. Jacob, when chosen by God did not know that I, God chose him, but he obeyed and moved away from the nation whose altar was an abomination to me. **Hosea 12:10-15.** It was for Jacob, just like I am telling you these. Jacob simple thought he was fleeing the wrath of his brother Esau and never knew it was among shepherds he was going to be a guest, let alone think of becoming a married man and a landlord, who would possess a great flock of livestock, since he was only a lad at that time. Jacob never thought he was going to travel so he would get himself prepared for it. If he had known his mother's counsel was going to breed a strife between him and his brother Esau, and cause him a flight, he would never have taken the mother's advice.

7. Look! Understand it that, it is I, Jehovah, who proves hearts and souls. The hidden fact in this matter is that, I observed in the heart of Esau that, he cherished the lifestyles of the nation whose traditions I hate and had purposed in his heart to marry his maiden of choice from among the nation whose activities stir my anger. If Esau married from among that nation, the seed of the family I intended to build for myself through my friend Abraham was going to mix up with the people of the world. **Genesis 26:34-35.** In spite of his parent's warning, he disobeyed and went ahead. While I waited, expecting he would probably change his mind on the wrong marriage, it was then that he affirmed his purpose by adding a second one to the earlier one to disrupt God's family. **Proverbs 12:21-22.**

8. I, Jehovah got very much peeved with this action of Esau so did I reject him and his generation for his

marriage did not follow my order. It was my spirit of instruction that urged their mother to offer the counsel that led to Esau being denied a blessing. Jacob did not know that God had chosen his family. When the enemy observed that, God's family would be a success through Jacob's marriage, it urged his master not to offer him the maiden for whom he had worshipped to be married. Jacob got bored by his action and wondered that his brother Esau had free hand in his marriage and married two easily. He contemplated leaving in anger and discarding the idea of marriage altogether, and thus becoming a nomad with no abode. All this while, Jacob never knew God's plan for him. I revealed myself to him and briefed him about my intention. **Isaiah 41:8-13.**

9. I caused all these words of blessing to manifest for Jacob, and so it is for you Victor also. Many fools have deserted you for the reason of my words

coming to you. After deserting you, they went to dead altars fooling themselves that Jehovah is in their midst. When I examined you, your altar and your chapel, it was observed that, we ought to come from heaven to give you strength so that you will have the same blessing from God. You children of today should therefore not be like Esau. **Hebrews 12:15-17.** It is never a good omen that befell Esau which should be repeated on others. It occurred to Esau as if it was the advanced age of his father that Jacob was able to dissuade him to bless him unawares. And since I wanted to reveal it to all generations that I caused it, I threw the anger in me against Esau on Isaac to curse him. **Genesis 27:30-41.** Esau thought it was his brother who through his wiles, took away his blessing, not knowing it was his waywardness in marriage that rather brought the curse on him.

10. Why should a young man decide to impregnate a lady outside the church and why should ladies of the church let themselves loose to wanton young men who cannot build a family for the God of Jacob? Look! All of you, members of this church should be very careful of yourselves. I Jehovah God, I continue calling families for myself. Why do people come to bow before my altar in worship but refuse to understand its worship precepts? **Malachi 2:15.** If those who gather in God's temple should have ulterior minds against each other and their young men would in treachery trail their ladies in false hearts, why then should they in pretense expose their nudity to outside ladies, faking holiness and stepping aside for the ladies in the church? Is it not the Lord's marriage order, which they have learnt and are conversant with that they are fleeing from?

11.   It is unto the outsider, who knows nothing about God's path of righteousness that they expose their nakedness. This is how I always advised my nation in the olden days and if they obeyed, they always enjoyed peace and blessing. I Jehovah God, while watching over all that is going on in the chapels on the earth, I observed that the spirit of the man of sin, which introduces vicious orders has filled all of them and the man of sin has sowed his seeds in all the patrons of the chapels. This is the spirit which has waged a way against all worships conducted in chapels on the earth, so has the prophecy in the scripture manifested on all the patrons of the chapels. **Hosea 4:12-14.** This passage testifies as to why God worshippers indulge in all sorts of corrupt lifestyles. But on the day that my spirit of vengeance shall rise, the whole world shall see it and shall be a true witness. The reason I am not meting out punishment to those believers who are practicing adultery and whoredom is that, it is

their priest who are leading the churches with corrupt doctrines.

12. They, with their hands institute orders and rules full of suppression and burden. When their members are unable to remain steadfast due to the weight of their rules, they turn into stealthy fornication and whoredom. This is the reason the Lord swore, if ever he will not avenge these leaders! **Isaiah 10:1-4.** It behooves priests to institute doctrines that will not lead the church members astray. Is it not the responsibility of the priests and the elders to ensure that marriage orders and their attendant rules are simplified for compliance in order to stem the tides of adultery and whoredom in the Church? It is written, the laws and the statutes belong to the priests. **Hosea 5:1-4.** Look! God's commandments and orders concerning marriage are those that give life to those who comply with them. Study the scriptures

critically from Moses into the prophets and you will have good understanding so that you don't go astray. **Malachi 3:22-24.** You must observe God's will so that you do not go astray. The covenant of I, Jehovah will not be broken. It must be clear to you that, it is in God's church that family is built for Jehovah. I declared that family be chosen for me in Isaac. **Romans 9:6-8.**

13. It is miserable to find people gathered in chapels without a family for God among them for nothing therefore do they gather in the name of God. I am The Ancient of Days and my words are not written to remain for nothing. **Isaiah 14:24-27.** I chose Isaac and so shall it remain forever and ever. Amen. The reason I chose Isaac is that, he humbled himself until his father got him a wife, so that he would not stray and get married in the wrong way. **Genesis 24:34-41.** Look! In the same way did I choose Jacob because he served Laban

until the father of the maidens offered them him. What then is happening among God worshippers today? Humans do not understand how I Jehovah created woman. All they know is that, the man was just there and I brought him the woman I created. I will explain woman's creation to you. Remember that, when the woman Isaac married, was brought to him, there were no days set aside as if to wait for any special rites before the woman becomes his wife. But as far as I God am concern, suitors must be taken through my rules and statutes before they can get into intimate relations as a couple.

14. What however is taking place viciously among God worshippers is the surprise, that the priest should in the presence of her parents offer their daughter to her suitor to become his wife without the witnessing of a marriage ring. Who gave God worshippers this vicious rule and which precepts of God approved of it before the majority of them are

practicing it? Look! They permit suitors to copulate and conceive, and some even give birth to all their children before setting aside a day of their choice to appear in God's presence for blessing. Who are these priests deceiving? Is it not written in the scripture that, "do not tread the path of Esau? **Hebrews 12:15-17.** I am the beginning and the end. I am making it clear to you that, it is not because of Esau's sale of his birthright that I hate him, and it is not he alone that I hate, but also his whole generation because of their excessive viciousness. **Revelation 2:6-7.** The spirit of deception has caused people to recall only his exchange of birthright with food, any time Esau's name is mention. But his adultery and his excessive lust after Hittite ladies and impregnating first before informing parents constitute the more reason, I hate him and his children because they are children out of wedlock. Esau's parents know it clearly that he will have no share in the family of God.

15.   Look! Do not be thinking about Esau's birthright which he had lost, but think rather about his adulterous ways in which he begot his children. I, Jehovah God, vowed that bastards will not get near my holy mount, and this started from Esau. **Obadiah 17:21.** The beneficiaries of all marriages taking place among patrons of chapels which are in semblance of that of Esau should know that, they and their descendants are just like Esau and his descendants. I, Jehovah the Almighty say so. Who can forestall what institute? Esau's parents are witnesses for I Jehovah in this case. **Genesis 26:34-35.** The reason I called his parents as witnesses is that, it is clear his parents never supported him in his adulterous marriage. They therefore warned him, but he never paid heed. This behaviour brought unto him and his descendants everlasting perdition. But I, Jehovah, I chose Jacob. Was it not the same father and mother who gave birth to Esau begot Jacob? The reason I chose Jacob is that, he obeyed his parents carefully and so when his

mother lamented to him about the Hittite girls, he obeyed. The obedience of Jacob to his parents drew I, Jehovah God close to him, to walk with him, since he obeyed them and never married any Hittite girl. **Genesis 27:41-46.**

16. Get it clearly that it was Jacob's own mother's relative, Laban's daughters he married as wives. He worshipped fourteen years to enable him marry the women. It behooves people to take good care, exercise patience like Jacob and get all dowry ready in proper order, through serious prayers. When you exercise enough restraint in marriage, you will be able to give the required attention to the woman. **Hebrews 12:7-8.** It has become the order of the day that people no longer pray for perseverance and self-control for steadfastness in temptations. This is the reason they engage in co-habitation, long before looking for time to come the presence of God. The way the man of sin meddles in

everything today to taint the glory of God's children, so was the deeds of the Hittite girls during Jacob's era. They exposed their nudity to the man they desired and if the man was not alert, he fell into their hand.

17. In the face of all female temptations, Jacob never went astray. What is so much difficult in your days presently, for which people cannot control themselves and remain pure for God? You must observe the self-control of Joseph, the earthly father of Jesus Christ. The young man, Joseph stayed in the same room with his wife Mary, but controlled himself to the extent that even with the sight of her nudity, he restrained himself and never had knowledge of her, whereas, in the consideration of humans, he could sleep with her because she was his wife. He revered God and controlled himself up to the time Mary had her first child. Learn from the sufferings and the long

suffering of your forebears, so that you don't get into the hands of the man of sin. The way I, Jehovah God created woman demands that, no one should just go in for her without my consent. Such actions bring much suffering and destruction into marriages of the sort.

18. I Jehovah created woman for the man and I possess the emotional control of every woman's heart. Amen! I turn a woman's heart and her love towards a man. As for men, they simply follow after a woman's beauty. A man is attracted by all the physical features of a woman and if a woman happens to expose her breasts or uncover any hidden part of her body, a man's heart is quickly turned, simply because of his eyes sight. The other issue to be observed is that, I steer off, a woman's love and her emotions from the man who is born out of the same womb with her, so they can stay together but cannot get married. There are men

whose sisters are more beautiful than their wives, but they labour a lot to satisfy the not so much attractive wives, for, it is the creation of I, Jehovah so that, one's sister will not drive his brother's wife away for not being beautiful. I created all women to be attractive, according to the different desires of the hearts of men.

19.   If a woman is said not to be beautiful, she probably will have male resemblance and if a man is said to be handsome, he may possess some female features. The commandment is that, one should not get married to the close relative because if this occurs, the emotive control will by all means switched off one day because a natural law has been flouted. **Genesis 18:6-18.** I decided that a man should respect his wife and offer her a position of honour. **Songs of Solomon 8:5-8.** The meaning of this scripture indicates that every man should present the woman he intends to marry to

God in the presence of his pastor, so the priest will pray and ask for peace upon the ring to be worn. Then will I, Jehovah God stir their love into full effect in them. If no emotive control proceeds from my spirit to bind the man's love to that of the woman, it would happen that one could be dispossessed of belongings and if this happens, the marriage will be rendered a mere mockery. This comes as a punishment to those who get married without remembering God.

20.   Some people receive this chastisement on earth. Luck befalls anyone who seeks refuge in God in all his ways. If a man should get his beloved wife in an illicit relation with another man, he could take his life without God's intervention when his love for her is so intense; to the extent that he would not think of the much sufferings after death. I guide those who find shelter in me and I become refuge for their souls. The spirit of God will not let a

faithful believer take his life for the reason of his wife's threats to divorce him. Jehovah will also not let a faithful believer get demented let alone become lunatic for his wife having divorced him or causing him some harm. It is the duty of I, Jehovah to take control of all these matters. If people would marry in accordance with God's orders the peace of my refuge will be among them and no one will get himself on the stake due to any serious crises.

21. I implore you all to turn to I, Jehovah God, so that I will be your refuge. There are men who have beautiful sisters but are unable to find suitable wives. So does it happen that some ladies may have handsome brothers but cannot find suitable men to marry them. It is I, Jehovah who causes all those to occur in their appropriate time. **Proverbs 19:14.** Pray for a change of mind if you are reading my commandments, so that the man of sin does not sow his seed of evil in you, for I, Jehovah have

purposed firmly that, no evil man will have my salvation. **Proverbs 1:23-33.** When I deploy my spirit of vengeance into the chapels, it will set aside all righteous people and will not do them any harm because they abide by my covenants, so it has become a refuge for them. That which happened in the olden days is what is happening today as well. **Ezekiel 14:12-23.**

Chapter 3

The Son represents the City of Refuge and abiding in the Son means living in the City of Refuge.

1. I am giving you emphatic confirmation that, I am The Ancient of Days and I do not change. The one who acknowledges me and forsakes his evil ways will have me as his refuge. The wanton spirit of heavenly hosts incited many of the people when I led my nation through Moses in the wilderness. **Acts. 7:42-45.** The activities of the worship of the heavenly hosts are so concealed that, if one does not turn unto God perfectly, such a one will be led by this spirit unawares. The first sign to notice if

such a spirit is leading a church is that, the members demonstrate an outward look as serious godly entrepreneurs, but their hearts and minds do not allow them to adhere to what they hear, let alone abide by them. Their daily lifestyles are never in tune with God's instructions. The particular sin they always confess is the one they commit repeatedly and confess. They never have control on sinful lifestyles for victory. According to the scriptures, however, one has to overcome the devil with the rightful gospel.

2. All worshippers ought to prove themselves with scripture and enquire how many will remain righteous should the scripture be used to give instant judgement? This is how these wanton spirits invaded the people in the wilderness and their confessions turned to enrage God. That which pleases I, Jehovah God about humans is for one to confess his sin and discard it. Better would be for

one, never to confess than to confess and baffle oneself and persist in it. If my spirit would terminate human race because of sin, it would not profit them. This is the reason I still keep my patience for humans to repent perfectly. **Job 34:10-16.** It is because of how peoples' confessions and atonements could not save them that I ordered Moses to select cities of refuge, into which sinners should flee in order not to die. For, people's actions make their sacrifices lose the potency of atonement. **Numbers 35:9-29.**

3. The cities of refuge were six, with three each on either side of the Jordan River. After Moses made the announcement and identified the cities, the nation got more strength to sin, since their confessions which exposed their stealthy deeds were no longer done. Thus, sins got heightened so much that I contemplated what to do for man to overcome sin. I came to realize that, the high

priests who liberated refuge seekers were also humans who committed sins and they also needed cities of refuge. Since I wanted to save the nation and deliver them from their sins and save the high priests, who were weakened under sin, I ought to change the priesthood. **Hebrews 7:26-28.**

4. Since it was heavenly hosts that changed into spirit and possessed the nation in the wilderness, it became imperative that the new high priest should also be spirit so he could deliver his nation from the unrighteous spirit. The anointed high priest was unable to deliver people from suppression. **Numbers 35:25-29.** What is more is that, murderers who fled to the cities of refuge were usually unable to abide by the rules of the cities and thus flouted them always. Now, the cities of refuge are in spirit and the High Priest in the spirit is the Son, Jesus Christ. There would not have been the need for the Son of God to die but because of

the law of the refuge cities' priesthood, Jesus ought to die, to be ordained as a high priest for refuge. The law provided that, if the anointed high priest died, then the murderer was absolved of his sins and should be pardoned.

5. Jesus became the high priest and He himself testified that the father sent Him. **Isaiah 61:1-3.** Concerning the spiritual cities of refuge, three witnesses ought to testify about the redemption of humans from sin and death. These witnesses are three on earth and three in heaven. These three testify that, the one who is anointed has died for the sins of God's nation. **I John 5:7-12.** I Jehovah, personally give this testimony about the Son, which signifies that, it is in the son that exist life and refuge for humans. The high priest, who is anointed with holy oil ought to enter His temple and perform his deliverance assignment. How is he going to dwell in the temple in which He Himself drew the

whip and drove people away? Is it not the things for which he drove the people away that are still going on in the chapels in our days? The priest ought to enter his temple, by all means, in order to make manifest the prophecy. The high priest, who is anointed with holy oil also needs to present himself to the temple and its patrons. This is the reason Jesus went into the temple.

6. It was the very day that Jesus presented himself in the chapel that I, Jehovah God changed the rules of the cities of refuge into those of the chapels. The words of atonement must manifest for the patrons of the chapels that have been built on these words of prophecy, so that those who will have shelter in God through their belief in them should be saved. I changed the covenant rules concerning the cities of refuge and ordered the Son to send the declaration into the chapels. **Isaiah 61:1-4.** The aim is to the manifestation of the temples becoming refuge to

people. However, the chapels are not able to save their patrons. The patrons of any places of worship which are unable to save them go astray through the search for other places of refuge and this is what is exactly occurring in these last days. Instead of the priests and prophets seeking after the reason the patrons of the chapels are denied perfect salvation, they are unable and rather have turned the chapels unto the search of survival. **Micah 3:5-12.**

7. Look! You will notice that, it is the very mistakes committed by the earlier generations that the present generations are also committing. I, Jehovah, know that this is because people do not really understand God before boasting of being men of God. It is because of these self-deceptive actions that I decided that the words of teaching should proceed from my mouth so, they will receive my messages and apply them to

understand the scripture, so people do not baffle themselves and go astray. **Malachi 3:22-24.** I keep sending prophets up till today, just as I did in the time of Elijah. I sent the Son to establish the refuge in chapels. But when the enemy realized that my intention was going to manifest through the efforts of the Son, he confused the order of the chapels, so that the places of worship will not serve a refuge for the people. This is the nature of the life-giving order; The high priest should fast, so that everything that he will ask in his prayers will remain an everlasting order. Since Satan knows that, food is indispensable for living, he came to tempt Christ with eating bread. **Matthew 4:1-4.**

8. Note it that, the tempter has planned to tempt every chapel and all places of worship with the temptations with which he tempted Jesus. If a gathering is not able to overcome the temptations, they get defeated and the devil tramples over

them. Any gathering which is unable to overcome temptation can also not be a refuge for any persons. The enemy's plan against the chapels is known to heaven, the reason for which the commandment that provides strength to the chapels started from the search for reward or food for oneself. **Matthew 10:8-10.** This rule as provided by the Son does not preclude caring for the needs of the workers of the sanctuary. Truly do I declare to you that no one can deny the servers of the sanctuary, their required reward. One however has to exercise great restraint in order to be able to overcome the snares set by the enemy against servers in the sanctuary, just like Jesus also persevered and overcome all his temptations.

9. The tempter will strike all who desire to overcome the snares of the enemy with the crises for physical needs. Be alert and hold onto the Son's instructions of remembrance in order to remain

steadfast. **Matthew 19:28-30.** The Son was tempted after His fasting prayers, but the enemy could not defeat him because there were none of his seeds in Him. In the same way should you also defeat the demonic ramifications of the enemy with your fasting and prayers. **Zechariah 8:14-17.** If in spite of your fasting prayers, you still conceal in your hearts the things I, Jehovah God hates, you are then supporting the enemy and your rejoicing will become teeth gnawing. The enemy has taken over the chapels for himself and has captured them through their search for bread and wages. My altars however exist with their orders and commandments. For you to defeat the enemy, you ought to understand that there is no food reward attached to the priesthood and altar of the Son. **Hebrews 13:9-10.**

10. Look! Any place that the order of the altar is changed to allow for wages and food, there is no

victory over the enemy. When they are overwhelmed by temptations, then the gathering is overtaken by pride and self-aggrandizement. The patrons of the chapels are filled with self-praise and the spirit of worldly success, so their souls become their captives. All their activities are geared towards the pleasing of men and not to please I, Jehovah. I declared firmly that Esau's way of marriage would not let him raise a family for Jehovah, However, it is Esau's way of marriage that is ruling among God worshippers today. **Malachi 1:1-5.** I know and continue to hear from the mouths of their priests and prophets, the promises of peace they pronounce on such evil marriages. But I am Jehovah and the person I am is what I remain to be. After they allow to be misled in their fleshly ignorance and after enjoying the pleasure of sin and revelry, I will chastise them in soul and spirit.

11. Whatever a man sows in flesh shall be reaped in soul and spirit. **I Corinthians 6:9-11.** I let Esau and Jacob reestablish peace with each other. I reestablish peace between Esau and Jacob, but how can there be peace between Esau and I? It is good for man to be in peace with his God. I want you to understand what I am telling you, that, it is good for man to establish peace with his creator, so, He will not be enraged against him and get him destroyed. **Zecheriah 1:1-6.** I declared that, man shall not live forever, so it is in his interest to turn away from evil before the end of his life is due. Look! Whatever worship a person practices has its mark on his soul, whether good or evil. This is why it behooves man to choose the worship in which he will be atoned for, so there will be peace between him and his creator. Look! There is no place where a human being will hide that is unknown to me. **Psalms 139:7-12.**

12. You seriously need to understand clearly, the scripture's pronouncement that "the first shall be

the last and the last shall be the first" That which is painful and should not happen to anybody, is what happened to Lot's wife Lot and his household had grace in my presence and I made him the proclaimer of righteousness in Sodom and its region. It happened that two young men of Sodom became suitors to Lot's two daughters. This marriage proposal made Lot's wife love to sound words of righteousness into the ears of the young men. The young men considered her a redeemed person as a result of her words of counsel. The angels who came to lodge with Lot did not also see any sign of perdition on the wife. This is because her efforts during their stay, her services and her relentlessness' in counseling the young men during their visit, all, served as an indication that the woman was far from perdition. Lot's wife was seen to have followed the husband on the day judgement and perdition approached, giving an assurance that they were not going to perish. Her steps did not demonstrate any sign of disobedience or destruction until they stepped out of the Sodom township. When destruction started, the two young men were involved.

13.   When Lot's wife's soul and the souls of the young men met after the destruction, they were astonished that the woman who taught righteousness was also among those who perished. The young men will regret their damnation, but Lot's wife's damnation is more regrettable because all her efforts have been rendered void. After I, Jehovah have contemplated the spouses of the altar worshippers, I observed that many of their wives are in the very footsteps of Lot's wife. All priests and prophets should apply the words of I, Jehovah to test their wives of their bosoms. Many of them are talkatives and do not know how to live in peace with each other. Be advised that, Lot did not let himself to be drawn into a fall by his wife. Even if the wife had cried out; the commandment

is "do not turn back". I counsel you, especially, servers of the altar that the wives of some of you are not conducting themselves in the manner befitting the spouses of priests. They can therefore lead their husbands into destruction. **Micah. 7:1-6.**

14. Dear colleague, be careful and alert if your wife praises you but insults the prophet and disdains other priests. I know the priests who give undue support to their wives and speak unedifying words about her colleagues as well as those who discuss the prophet. The colleague who does not advise his wife but allows her to counsel him into laziness and carefree life towards the worship should know that he is withdrawing his position from the midst of the lampstands. **Revelation   2:1-5.** Be firm and alert and do not let spousal love weaken the love for God in your souls. Each and every one should be careful of the wife of his bosom so that you do not make worthless efforts. **Micah 7:5-6.**

15. Watch against things that are abhorrent to me, so that you don't get involved with any of them in order not to desecrate your souls. I am the Ancient of Days. The person I hate because of his vicious lifestyles, I hate forever. When I decided to exterminate the people of Amalek, I sent King Saul to annihilate them. The King thought he could have mercy on them and his pity for them became a snare which trapped him and his family, so did King Saul and his children die in the same day. **I Sam. 31:1-6.** I, Jehovah crowned Saul as King over Israel, but he never obeyed my voice. Saul acted following his mind's conception without seeking my advice. The reason I gave Saul and his household out to his enemies to kill is this: Saul got enraged against my priests but did not restrain himself to seek the opinion of I, the one who made him King before using his anger. He caused the death of eighty-five of the priests of I, Jehovah, ordered the demolition of my temple and burnt the homes of my priests.

16. What crimes did the priests commit against Saul? He required from them to apply their priestly powers to show him where David was hiding, and wanted their priestly support to kill David. The priests, after pondering over the king's request decided that, it was not proper for priests to support murder and they should not shed innocent blood. When the king realized that the priests did not accept his request and support his evil counsel, he killed all of them. **I Samuel 22:17-33.** What enraged me the more about Saul is that, he did not want to destroy Amalek. The nation I accursed because of their evil nature was the one he rather had pity for and hardened his heart and killed the priests of Jehovah; the servers of my altar who were blameless in the eyes of I, Jehovah God. Get it clear that, it was not his refusal to exterminate Amalek that was the only fault of Saul; I could have had mercy on him. But now that he has killed my

priests, I ought to avenge the blood of my priests and my anointed.

17. Look! I am Jehovah and I never change. One who does not revere me afflicts himself for nothing. I said I hate Esau, and not he as an individual but mean all his generation. **Obadiah 6:10.** I am Jehovah and I hate wicked actions. I made you understand why I hate Esau and his way of marriage cannot raise a family for me. King Saul also did not deserve to live and be wicked to my priests: so did I exterminate him and his household. If somebody will lead his life with things that are abhorrent to God, Jehovah will reject and hate him. if men went astray and tempted God with what He abhors and perished, why then should this latter generation expect in their hearts that God will not punish the wayward? Verily do I declare to you that, since the era of Moses, whoever flouted any of the laws died without mercy. **Hebrews 10:26-31.**

18. If you really understand the scriptures, it would have been very difficult for your enemy to deceive you, let alone capture you. The commandments of the Son of God are easier than those of Moses. However stiffer punishments await those who flout the laws of the Son of God. Those who exchange the laws and orders of the Son of God with their own will should expect God's vengeance. Some people sometimes change the time of the orders of the Son of God with their own will for their self-praise from people. The quest for praise from people has led many believers astray from the truth. Be careful of the quest for praise from people. If you please people, you cannot please God. **Galatians 1:10.** Let it be clear to you that the desire to please humans allows spiritual exposures, which lead people into being withdrawn from the faith. Pleasing humans could not let somebody prefer to attend a funeral rather than to go to worship on Jehovah's altar. The worship of people,

who exchange funeral and revelry with the service periods of God is before my eyes like funeral meals, defiled with corpses. **Hosea 9:4-5.**

19.   The question is asked that; do all God worshippers rally in the proper order into God's house on the occasions during which worshippers are expected to rally? When people exchange God's days of sacrifice with things they think are important to them, and later come to bow before I, Jehovah, their worship is like unto funeral meals desecrated with corpses. Such people will call God in their times of crises, but Jehovah God will not hearken unto their prayers; because they do their own things on God's days of repose. The one who will call me and I will respond and remain his God is the one who pays attention to my inscriptions and abides in them. These are the type of people whose worship pleases me. **Isaiah 56:1-2.** Humans ought to know that, the purpose of what has been

written down is for it to be read, so it will show the pathway of light to life, to avoid going astray. Those whose prayers I am pleased with are those who do not take over God's days and periods of repose for themselves, but they rather put aside their own things and observe God's days as special. **Isaiah 56:6-8, Isaiah 58:13-14.**

20. Satan, your enemy knows that, people lack perfect understanding of the scriptures; the reason for which he has courage to imbibe people with ulterior understanding. If you will turn unto the scripture and ask for the spirit of perfect understand of them, the enemy would never conquer you. Look! It is imperative for you believers to apply the work of faith to resemble the Son, so that you will by all means possess His very image. **I Corinthians 15:45-49.** It is the reserved will of I, Jehovah to reveal mysteries to you. Look! The sufficiency of the Godhead is accomplished in the

Son. **Colossians 1:16-19.** This mystery commenced in heaven and is established that the Son got begotten before all the principalities that exist in the heavens and that all principalities that will exist in the Son's Kingdom must resemble the Son in everything. All things started from the high priest Melchizedek in heaven. Many archangels existed, but when the lot was cast, it fell on Melchizedek, for the reason of him taking the first position in resembling the Son of God. The fact exists that, other archangels also resemble the Son but the testimony of Melchizedek by far surpasses all in resembling the Son in all things. This is the reason he was given the office of the everlasting high priest. **Hebrews 7:1-3.**

21.   It pleases heavenly powers that whoever will resemble the Son or put on his likeness should be a member of the congregation of the high priest, Melchizedek. The commandment is that, all who

will proclaim Melchizedek in any instance must resemble the Son in lifestyle, steps and speech. If one does not resemble the Son, but knows the name Melchizedek and proclaims it incessantly, that person is deceiving himself. The rule dictates that one must resemble the Son in order to receive an instant response when He is called upon. Let everyone examine himself very well to see if he resembles the Son. Does your speech resemble that of the Son? Do you tread the footsteps of the Son in your everyday life? **I John 3:1-3.** The order permits that whoever shall endeavour to resemble the Son is already registered as a member of the heavenly congregation in spirit. The support heaven provides for the believer who abides in God is that the Son of God has been brought on earth for him also to dwell in the world, so that, whoever shall believe and partake in the body of the Son and drink of His blood through faith, shall be changed to resemble the Son of God. The Son of

God ought to resemble His fellows and his fellows also resemble Him. **Hebrews 2:16-18.**

22. Just as it is an order in heaven to resemble the Son in order to obtain the position a high priest, so has heaven also decided that whoever shall become an everlasting high priest for humans on earth should be subdued below an angel's status in order to resemble the people he will be serving. **Hebrews 2:5-9.** There has been attempts to get an everlasting high priest for humans among arch angels in heaven, but because their submission could not equal that of the Son, He became a Victor for having been humbled to the status of a human being. **Philippians 2:5-11.** The scripture indicated that, He discredited Himself, an action which other angels attempted but were unable to achieve. It is only the Son, who was able to achieve this, the reason for which He was declared in heaven as the priest in the priestly order of Melchizedek.

Hebrews 7:14-17. It is not the importance of His priesthood that matters, but that, it is the order of everlasting life which was incorporated into his priesthood that made Him surpass all, with the understanding that, whoever shall resemble the Son in all things shall have the gate of everlasting life opened for him, for it is in the vow of Jehovah that the everlasting life made its passage through the Son for the whole world. **I John 5:11-13.**

23. The devil, having observed that humans will have eternal life through resembling the Son, he endeavours to change himself in the likeness of the Son. He attempts to resemble the Son outwardly but can never change his inward nature to resemble him. Faithful believers ought to be alert to identify the dragon which changed itself into the likeness of the Son by its speech. **Revelation 13:11.** I must reveal one more mystery to you before concluding the message about the dragon. It is the

believers who conquer the beast and the dragon that shall eat of the victors' bread and drink of the cup of the conquerors. For someone to be in the conqueror's fellowship, he ought to learn the vow of conquerors by its content and conduct himself with it in a perfect manner. You ought to learn the conqueror's vow and master its words perfectly in the church. **Psalms 101:1-8.**

24. Jesus, the Messiah was able to conduct his life with the words of this psalm 101. If the scripture makes reference to a governor's vow, who then do you consider as the ruler? I affirm to you that, whoever shall believe in the Son and change his lifestyle to resemble that of His, such a one shall be the conqueror. I the Ancient of Days have enough courage that, if these mysteries shall be explained to you, you will love to learn them and become conquerors by mastering them. The message declared by the Son to his disciples on the day of

the unleavened bread is a great promise. Jesus' proclamation that "I shall not drink of the vine until you and I shall drink of the newness in my Father's Kingdom", is a viable promise. Understand it that, it is the blessed body of Christ that will help believers to become conquerors by partaking in His flesh.

25. The one who sacrificed His flesh and blood for the remission of sin among humans cannot eat His own flesh and drink His own blood. It has been testified elsewhere about the Son that, He is a human being who never knew any sin, and lies have never been heard in His mouth, but He rather shed His blood for the remission of sins. What Jesus meant by the proclamation: "you and I shall drink in newness in heaven" refers to the drink of rulers and the meal of those who overcome temptations. Jesus overcame all His temptations and is therefore seated on the right hand of the Father, waiting for other overcomers, so as to set before them the

overcomers' table. It is overcomers who shall sit by the table and eat and drink in the presence of I, Jehovah on my Holy Mount. **Isaiah 25:6-9.** Look! It is important that you pray and understand Jesus' instructions, otherwise, Satan will defeat you because of your lack of understanding. The one who is without sin cannot apply His own blood on Himself. The drinking of a new wine refers to the overcomers' position Jesus has attained.

26.   The person who takes the communion according to its perfect order is the one who endeavours to be one of the overcomers. For one to be sure he is in the fellowship of the overcomers, he needs to examine his daily life with the full content of Psalm 101, and when he is found to tread accordingly, he will by all means become an overcomer, as is indicated by the title of the Psalm. Since the disciples Jesus chose for his ministry of grace did not understand most of His

teachings, Satan fought them and they suffered many crises. This is how Satan desires today, that worshippers should not understand the scriptures, so he will use their ignorance to capture them with ease.

27.   The Son asked His disciples whether they understood His teachings. He knows very well that, if someone does not understand something before going to do it, he falters by all means. They answered Him that they understood them, meanwhile it was not all of them who understood. **Matthew 13:47-52.** The scripture likens the kingdom of heaven to a net, cast into the sea, which caught both edible and inedible fish. It could be that, it is not all the fishes drawn ashore that the fisherman wants. Many may be needless to him but the net brought them ashore. It now behooves the fisherman to apply a lot of patience and select his preferred fish for which he cast the net. This is the

nature of priesthood assignments. It is not all members of the church that are God's chosen ones and it is not on the chosen ones alone that the priest should labour. Just as the inedible fishes adds to the weight of the net but the fisherman pulls all with all his strength, so is the church. Fishers could not have gone under the sea to remove the inedible fishes from the net before pulling the net ashore.

28. The weeds are overpowering the millet since they do not understand the message in order to comply with it; but Jesus did not permit the uprooting of the weeds. Being together always; all that the millet needs to do to overcome the weeds is to fully understand the messages, so God's realization will let the word overcome on their behalf. Hear this: I am Jehovah, the creator of heaven and earth. As I have not created the earth to remain barren, but I filled it with humans and

living creatures, so do I declare to you with emphasis that, I did not create heavens to remain empty, but I promised it to humans for inheritance. Amen! **Matthew 5:10-12.** So do I promise humans who are pure in their hearts that they shall see me; Jehovah with their naked eyes. **Matthew 5:8.** Let me explain to you the reason I caused the man Paul to be brought to the third heavens to you, an action which opportunity the disciples of Christ never had. **II Corinthians 12:1-7.**

Chapter 4

Practicing Christ in the power of the Holy Spirit conquers fear and ensures steadfastness.

1.   Paul testified about the need to labour relentlessly about the gospel's ministry and how it is possible to be taken to heaven in accordance with the promise. It is a fact that Paul was not part of the twelve disciples. The disciples of Jesus were always with Him while he was in flesh on earth, and they had all hope in Him as their powerful master. This made them all subjects to "seeing is believing". They always relied on the body of Jesus, so anytime He was not with them physically, they were always very much afraid. This made Satan strike them with

the spirit of fear. Pray to be purged of the spirit of fear, so as to receive the power of the Holy Spirit, to be imbued with its might. The promise is that: "You shall receive the power of the Holy Spirit. **Romans 8:15-17.**

2. Satan knew very well that the commandments of the covenant have been changed and accomplished in the Holy Spirit. He also knew that the physical body of Jesus was to be taken to heaven and the one upon whom the disciples would rely in their ministry would be wanting. While I, Jehovah studied the disciples, I did not find one whose faith was perfectly steadfast. They all had their faith leaning on Jesus. The faith which leans on someone else works imperfectly, the reason for which the scripture provides that: "blessed be the one who does not see but believes". **Hebrews 11:1-3, II Corinthians 5:7-9, John 20:27-29.** Look! These were the scriptures

Satan used to charge the disciples of Jesus on the Mount of Congregation. It behooves you believers to be alert because the accuser of your colleagues is still at work. There was nothing I, Jehovah could do about the weakness of their faith after Satan came to accuse the disciples. Look! If somebody's faith is exhausted, the person is separated away from heaven, because faith is the bridge by which heaven communicates with humans. The disciples testify asking Jesus to support their faith because their faith was exhausted; since it was built on the physical body of Jesus. Jesus used to advise his disciples serially to build their faith on spiritual things, because, if what they see is carried away, their faith would as well be carried away. The faith needs to be built on the spiritual things of God in order to remain strong. **II Corinthians 4:16-18.**

3. Satan observed Jesus' disciples to have gone astray in the matter of faith and was therefore in

wait patiently that the day Jesus will be carried away from them, he will descend into their midst in the church in Jerusalem and fight with them since the power of their faith has been taken away. The problematic fact that caused the spirit of Jesus not to perform mighty works in the first church of Jerusalem was their lack of faith, which made the church not pleasing to God. **Hebrews 11:6.** This made Satan shake the church with threats. Satan caused Stephen to be executed in the glare of the church as a measure to frighten believers to not proclaim the name of Jesus. But before his death, heaven encouraged him to speak to his murderers to see if they would probably change their mind and spare his life. **Acts. 7:49-53.** I made Stephen remind them that, they had built a temple for me but it is surprising that it was the patrons who were killing God's saints.

4. In like manner was it on the day Jesus was tried; the governor and his officials decided to acquit Him but it was the worshippers of God, who cried at the top of their voice to the governor to crucify him. This is how Satan captures people in the church, to the extent of inciting church members to even kill them. Woe betides those who receive such demonic powers from Satan for the destruction of the members of God's church. I, Jehovah will personally fight them. We are going to get at war to see who will be able to destroy the other. It is peace that I have purposed for you humans, so do I advise the offspring of the serpent to seize this opportunity to learn to make peace. **Isaiah 27:1-6.** The peace about which the scripture speaks will be manifest for the righteous by all means Even if the offspring of the serpent advance into dragon, I Jehovah will keep watch over the whole church.

5. All my spirits of witnessing which came to teach you have observed this fault of leaning the faith on humans in many, many of you in the church. Some people have in their spirit selected some leaders for themselves and others love some leaders more than others. The question poses itself that. If the leader your faith leans on or you love is no more, or if he backslides and leaves the church, will he not go along with your faith? There are leaders among you, who pray with much seriousness and courage, but many for whom they pray dislike them or rather their hearts are attached to some other leaders who may not be caring in such prayers. This type of weak faith was found among the earlier believers the reason for which Satan scattered them. I advise you to be affable to each other and avoid offending each other so that Satan does not accuse you. Satan made a lot of threat with Stephen's death.

6. The only thing that can stop this threat posed by Satan is abiding in the faith that has no leaning on a human being. The faith that entertains no doubts and has no fears for spiritual things is required for people to be able to continue the work. The Disciples of Christ were afraid and lamented a lot and the occurrence of Stephen's death without the intervention of Christ to save him got the disciples scattered. The fact that they got scattered, as well as their ignorance about the default of their faith left them in a position in which they could not repair their stand for heaven to intercede on their behalf. This gave Satan a lot of happiness about their weakness. Satan is very much empowered if he observes a believer to be leaning his faith on a human being. **2 Corinthians 5:14-17.** Repose your faith on the spiritual renewal of the Holy Spirit. The scripture declares that, you are being led by the love of Christ, which is His spirit and it is not declared that Christ will descend into your midst with His physical body. If you don't see Christ with

your naked eyes, but you believe in Him, then you are in the faith that draws down the power of heaven in total fullness; therefore, maintain your stance. **I Peter 1:8-11.**

7. This is how your saintly forebears prayed these matters into detail and desired to know how the Church of Christ was going to fare, if the Lord had left the world. They also probed into how a man was going to fare if his faith and hope were placed on what cannot be seen with the naked eye. They still probed further that, how were the churches going to have their faith reposed in Christ, if Jesus was not going to remain on earth physically? Now, if Jesus was going to send a spirit to the churches on earth, how was this spirit going to be like? If the spirit arrives, what type of glory will He lead the people into? After deeply probing into these, they came to the realization and the testimony that; all the things were accomplished in the spirit and that

if Christ's spirit dwells in a person, then that person is a child of God. **Romans 8:9-14.**

8. The faith of the disciples was attached to the body of Christ and it is this body that has been taken to heaven. It now became clear that, as a result of fear, the disciples were not going to be able to establish the new covenant, whereas it was upon it the spirit of Christ resides. Then heaven observed that, Satan realized that the nation revered Saul and honoured him greatly, and because of his advanced education, the disciples feared him more than the governors. This Saul was greatly pleased with Stephen's death. **Acts 7:56-59.** It was notices from heaven that; Satan used the fickle faith of the disciples to drive them into hiding. Satan then started charging the disciples with the charges that were used to accuse Jesus so that they could be arrested and killed. **Acts 6:11-15.** It was the charges upon which Stephen was

killed that Saul armed himself with, holding the intention that, if any of Christ's disciples should flee to any of the neighbouring kingdoms, he will provide the governors with the same charges, so that the disciple will be given out and killed. Saul got informed that, some of them had fled to the city of Damascus.

9. Now, if heaven should wait for the disciples to get awaken and realize the need to amend the stand of their faith to be able to withstand Saul, Satan would have by then been too much empowered. Then heaven went into counsel and God's Wisdom declared that; this Saul ought to be captured for God's mission – and the whole of heaven was pleased with this advice. In that very hour Saul was heard in heaven praying, asking God to give him the wisdom and skill to be applied to arrest the destroyers of the temple of Jerusalem. It was on his way to Damascus that Jesus revealed His

glory to him. Satan had imbued Saul with bravery, wickedness and a ruthless heart and was sure Saul would never, never change. Then God's Wisdom made him blind and he could not see. God's Wisdom struck his companions with fear and they fled. **Acts 9:1-9.** They observed that, they did not know what would happen to them, if the continued to stay with him, they therefore abandoned him and went back to Jerusalem and narrated the incident in the city and its neighbourhood.

10. Great fear befell Jerusalem and its inhabitants as a result. When Saul's parents and family heard about his plight, they sent emissaries to go and bring him home. It took the emissaries two days to get to Damascus. When they asked about Saul from some of the inhabitants, they know nothing about him. When they asked of him by asking about some priests, they were finally brought into the house, where Saul was residing. **Acts 9:10-15.** Saul's

relations wanted to take him away, but Ananias told them that; "there lies the man; seek his view to follow you, if he agrees". Since Saul was by then blind, they got scared and thought he could be left blind if they forced him. They therefore left him without arguing with him. They left with the understanding that; Ananias should heal him before they come for him. After the departure of the relatives, God's Wisdom fell on Ananias to heal Saul and open his eyes. **Acts 9:17-19.**

11. Saul's relatives were frightened, more so, when he was not eating, but after hands were laid on him, his eyes opened and he ate and drunk. Heaven considered his three days without food as the sign of the Son of Man. **Matthew 12:38-40.** Saul remained without food for three days and three nights. Jonas also stayed in the belly of a whale for three days and three nights. This was a sign of repentance, but Saul went through this without the

realization, because he himself did not know that he had been chosen for any special ministry. When his relatives heard that he had been healed but he did not attempt to come back to Jerusalem, they again sent after him to Jerusalem. When they met him, they briefed him about developments and informed him that the high priests and the scribes were expecting him in Jerusalem.

12. Saul answered them that, he had been captured by the hands of the Jesus, whom he had been persecuting, but he did not kill him as he had seen doing to people who believed in him, and that, his spirit had not permitted him to go back to his family. They asked him, "What is the spirit?" They were astonished, and what even made them believed that he was getting out of his senses was when he told them that, the spirit has changed his name to be called Paul. They also noticed that his pronouncements were also in support of the

disciples of Jesus. This development surprised them and they left for home in anguish. Great fear befell the whole of Jerusalem and its inhabitants due to these issues and no one had any more courage to persecute the disciples. After Saul's vision, which opened his eyes, he realized that, he was going to be taken to the midst of the disciples, whom he used to persecute, he therefore laid his faith and hope on the vision. It was with great courage that he went into the house of Ananias. He thought Ananias would query him, accuse him and expose him to a lot of harm.

13. It however did not happen as he thought, but Ananias received him with courage and let him stayed with him in peace. Ananias did not avenge him for his wicked acts. This resulted into Paul confessing his sins and he prayed for him. After Paul's confession and Ananias' prayers for him, heaven considered the prayer accompanied by

confession as a perfect sacrifice. **Acts 9:10-19, Psalms 66:16-20.** It behooves believers to do confessions out of faithful heart, and all confessants must discard all evil for perfect remission. This is how heaven has been since the olden days and does not change. **Ezekiel 33:14-16.** Oh, Son of man, understand it that your peace and victory reside in the confession and the discarding of all evil. I am the Ancient of Days. Your forebears had peace and victory after they confessed their sins and desisted from them. This is what is required of you also, in these end times.

14. Paul's confession was not mere verbal pronouncement but he acted according and his testimonies gave confirmation to the unbelievers that Paul really repented and changed. **Acts 9:20-25.** What offered more hope to the heavens about him was the conspiracy of the Jews to kill him, which did not frighten him, even with the threat of

death. After heaven observed that his confession was perfect and was not a mere pronouncement, he was approved as their colleague. I am now going to speak to you about the requirements for the establishment of the new covenant. Look! I am that which I am. If I, Jehovah decide something, there is none that can change it. Before a place is found for the new covenant on earth and among humans on earth there is the need to have someone who will be able to teach and his teaching should offer humans the understanding to agree to discard the first covenant and receive the second one, due to the weakness in the first one. **Hebrews 8:6-7.** Though this second covenant was firmly established in heaven even on the Mount of Congregation, it has not yet gotten a place among humans on earth.

15. This made Satan thought with courage that, humans have no knowledge about the new

covenant. It is imperative that humans understand this covenant well and deliver their souls by complying with it. This covenant will also not be effective unless certain aspects of the old ones were changed before the new one is able to fully establish and work. **2 Corinthians 3:12-18.** Just as the old covenant is wholly human instruction, so is the new covenant also wholly spiritual teaching. Just as the two covenants proceed from one God, so are the two concealed in Jesus the one Son of God in their ministry in the world. People believed in Jesus because they witnessed his ministry eye to eye. **John 4:39-42.** It is in this same Jesus that resides the spiritual commandment, which is the new covenant and it behooves humans to discard the physical things of Christ and turn unto the things of His spirit, because, it is written that: "the flesh profits nothing but the spirit quickens", therefore, seek after the spirit of Jesus and things in it. **2 Corinthians 5:14-17.**

16. For a person to become a new creation, he ought to be taught with the covenant of the spirit with sufficient courage, to be able to discard the old-thing and turn unto the new one. For example, the use of the infant history of Jesus, his death on the cross and his rising as a festival has nothing near the spirit of Jesus in any way. **Hebrews 6:1-2.** It is only when the spirit of Jesus enters someone that the person can be raised from among the dead. Without the spirit, no dead human can be resurrected. The spirit of Jesus must resurrect whoever believes in Jesus into life from among the dead. **Romans 8:8-11.** It must be clear to you this way: All the disciples of Jesus, who stayed with him and knew him physically, eye to eye did not have the strength of faith in the spirit in its fullness. Paul, who never stayed anywhere with him while he was in flesh but had the shine of the glory of His spirit on the way to Damascus was the one who accomplished the commandment of faith in its

perfect form, for he never saw any image on which to build his faith, but the spirit.

17. He did not see anything, but was strengthened by the confirmation of faith from the spirit. When heaven saw his position of faith, they obtained enough courage about him. He was then to start his missionary work. All this while, Paul never had any short comings, which needed a consultation from the disciples, to enquire about this or that, with the understanding that, they had stayed with Jesus and worked with him face to face. Paul never needed any advice from the disciples of Jesus in any instances, but rather, it was the disciples who sometimes enquired to understand certain things from him, having learnt how the spirit transformed him for special assignments. **Acts 13:1-3.** This is the special ministry. The Old Testament offers the understanding regarding the covenant of circumcision between God and humans. There is

the need for the proclamation to humans to put their faith away from this commandment of physical covenant and proclaim that people should receive the circumcision of the spirit. **Romans 2:28-29.**

18. Satan got himself ready against anybody who will proclaim this new change to be killed. This is where Jesus' disciples got into serious fears. Peter, who Jesus declared as the rock on which to build His church also had the spirit of fear, so did heaven not establish the new covenant on him. It was because of fear that Peter denied knowledge of Jesus since he feared the circumcised sect. **Galatians 2:1-2.** Now, if Peter is unable to proclaim the transformation in the new circumcision and no one is found capable of making this proclamation, then it means that, the new covenant has no place among humans. Paul is one person, who Satan could not defeat with fear in order to prevent him

from making his proclamation. So through his relentless efforts and effective proclamation, the circumcision in the new covenant appealed to people's heart and got established.

19. The Godhead decreed on the Mound of Congregation that, there was the need to find a person, born of humans on earth, who could do the proclamation, and if the new covenant is to be established, such a one should be permitted to be carried into heaven to go and see the place prepared for his soul; the place prepared for him because of his efforts. This is how Paul was taken to heaven. **2 Corinthians 12:1-10.** His proclamations and relentless efforts requested that people should discard the sacrifices of animal blood in accordance with the new covenant and believe in the sacrifice of the blood of Jesus Christ. Paul obtained a lot of courage in the spirit and made many people repent from the sacrifice of animal

blood and established the faith of the church on the belief in the blood of Jesus. This also got a place among humans. **Hebrews 10:1-10.** Paul explained these things into detail to the nation and it is a perfect truth that it was through Paul that the transformation that came through the new covenant was established among humans. The seeing is believing faith which the disciples had caused Satan to tie them up seriously with the fear for death.

20. Then Peter applied a lot of tact to let people know that Paul was ordained for the uncircumcised, the reason for which he teaches about uncircumcision. He again made them aware that, it was also for the heathen that he was ordained, but he, Peter was ordained only for the Jews. Peter, therefore, with tact fled the rancor of the establishment of the new covenant. **Galatians 2:6-10.** Satan fought seriously with the disciples of

Jesus and he applied fear to weaken them and thus prevented heaven from their new covenant. When the need arose for the establishment of the Holy Communion, it was Paul that heaven used but not Peter who had witnessed its physical occurrence during the time of Jesus. **I Corinthians 11:23-34.** After Satan realized that, there was nothing he could do about Paul, he decided to attempt his fall through his marriage affairs, so that he would lose his position as offered him in heaven. Satan fought Paul seriously with the demonic spirit called the man of sin. This spirit deceived many of the elders of the church, who used to help Paul and they fell from their position of eldership, leaving Paul all alone. **2 Timothy 1:15-18.**

21. Satan incited some of Paul's church elders and got them fallen with the lust for the pleasure of maidens. There was an attractive lady in the house Paul used to lodge on whom Paul's heart

sometimes turned, and he used to think about how the lady used to take good care of him. This is how some people even came to think that Paul had a wife in that house. Satan later decided to use the lady to trap Paul. It did happen that very night that, Paul's persecutors came and arrested him, jailed him, with the intention to kill him. **Acts 23:12-16.** One other fact Satan stood against seriously, for which he wanted to kill him was his knowledge of the fact that he was to be taken into the glory of heaven. You will notice this arm of viciousness, that when Paul was a young man, who ignorantly received the power of wickedness from Satan, he at that time did not want him killed but he used him to kill others. What good reward did Paul get while he worked for him by then?

22. But when the glory of heaven shone on him now, he became his bitter foe, and he desired to apply unrighteous means to kill him. Heaven used

to keep watch over him, on occasions where he nearly showed weakness in the missionary work, heaven strengthened weakness in the missionary work, heaven strengthened him through visions. **Acts 18:9-13.** Paul was on several occasions accused of teaching different things in place of the old covenant, which he knew very well. The name I gave him at that time was: Fear Not I am with you". The power of this name and its realization is in the church under you. I counsel you all to learn these words which are messages of the heavenly powers. They are the words of promise which have been in existence since the time of old, as have been recorded, so that the church will receive the power of the heavens. **Ephesians 1:1-4.** It was the blessings of heaven and their powers that strengthened Paul and the people of his time, and it is with this same power that I am advising you, the believers of the present day.

23. Heaven was waiting for Paul to be carried away after his persecution, in accordance with his measure of glory. The lady who used to get close to him was still around, and whilst he, never knew that she was being used as a trap against him maintained his affable stand. When heaven realized that the woman was going to get him fallen, Satan was permitted to strike him with nasty rashes all over the body. **2 Corinthians 12:6-9.** He never knew he was being prepared to be taken to heaven through that bodily affliction. The fifth of the rashes did not endear him to many of his friend any longer but Paul fought night and day with prayers. While he had no healing, his mind took him into wandering frequently. Though his mind told him on occasions that God had rejected him, he never stopped praying, and while people deserted him, he never stopped praying and while he was still alone, he still held onto faith and courage. **2 Timothy 1:15-18.** In this long suffering

and submission, he was permitted to be taken to the third heaven. **2 Corinthians 10:1-3.**

24. The great humility found in Paul compelled I the Ancient of Days to order him to be carried to heaven. **2 Corinthians 12:1-5.** I am Jehovah, and I am that which I am. If I plan something, who can change it? It was during Paul's passage to heaven that he learnt about priesthood and it was in this vision that he heard all about the high priest Melchizedek. He learnt a lot of things in this vision, which were unknown to the disciples of Jesus. It was in heaven here that his mind got opened and he was offered the grace not to forget the things he had witnessed in heaven and that his mind and memory should be alive so that he would be able to write them, to make humans aware of the mysteries. He really wrote adequately about the heavenly priesthood. **Hebrews 7:1-7.** Through his acquired humility, he was permitted by heaven to

know a lot of spiritual mysteries, which knowledge never occurred to any of the disciples of Jesus. It was in heaven here he was taught how to establish the order of celebrating the Holy Communion as well as correcting many more worship orders. **I Corinthians 11:17-34.**

25.   Paul was endowed with the power from heaven to correct things because he was the only apostle, who had the courage and did not fear the threats posed by the Jews. He established the new covenant and proclaimed that; it should be applied in all places of worship in the established order. Heaven testified about him as to how he endeavoured to transform the commandments and the orders to conform to the order of the new covenant. When his life was threatened for teaching about the needlessness of circumcision, heaven protected him from his enemies. **2 Corinthians 11:26-33, Acts 9:20-25.** Look! Victor,

from where will reward come for the person who sacrificed his life for the heavenly Kingdom and its righteousness? Will that not by all means proceed from heaven? From where will consolation come for such people, if not heaven? Look! The disciples of Jesus endured sufferings for the gospel, but I declare to you that, Paul's efforts for sowing the seed of the gospel surpassed the efforts of the disciples several fold. So does every good labourer receive his deserved reward. It was this same Paul heaven used to transform the rules of marriage and got them firmly established. **I Corinthians 7:10-11.**

Chapter 5

Alertness with the mind of Christ sustains faith defeats the minds of men that lead into waywardness.

1. In respect of the commandment about marriage, Paul ought to have spoken only about the instructions given him by the Lord, but because the enemy fought him in his mind, he was able to state that, he Paul as flesh said so. **I Corinthians 7:12-15.** Think properly about Paul's case and you will realize that he set his conviction as a rule. Look! The commandment which brings everlasting life is the one established that: From the beginning of things, they were created husband and wife. **Matthew 19:1-11.** If Adam divorced his wife, where was any other woman for him to marry? The most

important aspect of the order that existed from the beginning is that: "What God has put together, no one should put asunder". Paul spoke the truth that he had received from heaven that, the law is for the married couple to know. The law did not refer to the couple who are believers, all alone. Let it be clear to you that marriage is about the multiplication of generations and is not a preserve to being a believer. Adam and Eve were not members of any church during their life time. Marriage is older than church membership. It was the same Paul, who taught that couples should not divorce each other, who immediately after then laid emphasis on being a believer and stated that, if it did not please anyone to maintain the marriage, they could divorce. **I Corinthians 7:12-15.**

2. Be careful about the 15th verse because it is the source of confusion in marriage. Consider the fact that, Paul declared that, it was not the commandment of the Lord. Which one will you

comply with? Is it that of the Lord which does not come from the weakness of the flesh or the fleshy one of Paul, which is completely weak into condemnation? I, am waking you up unto the statements of Paul in order to remain alert, so that you do not practice the order of the flesh and abandon that of the spirit, which gives life.

3. The enemy's fight against prophecy receivers is in many ways. This is what happened to Paul, and if you Victor do not exercise sufficient care, it will happen to you also. Peter was first to notice Paul's teachings, for they got mixed up with heavenly teachings and if one does not remain alert, he could be led astray. **2 Peter 3:14-16.** It does not matter for any natural cause, if a believer decides to marry an unbeliever. They were simply husband and wife in the beginning. It could happen that an unbelieving wife could cause the backsliding of a believer husband and he will lose his soul. In the same way, if a believer woman decides to marry an unbelieving husband, she must be getting herself ready for falling out of the faith. Every marriage has its share of temptation, but a couple who are believers are more likely to overcome temptations

than others. It is easier withstanding crises when both are members of the same faith than when they are on separate axis the people who worship on the same altar that fellowship together. Birds of the same feathers flock together. **I Corinthians 10:15-18.**

4. The wise ones among you should understand this and learn how to marry their spouses, so that they are not driven into mishap. Paul had enough grace and possessed much heavenly mysteries. **Ephesians 3:1-7.** As a result of he having received much divine mysteries, the enemy usually trailed Paul and most of the times attempted to land him in trouble. He came to notice that, he could not have been taken to heaven if he had been married. Having had this realization, he got convinced that, it would be good if people remained single like him. **I Corinthians 7:7-9.** It pleased Paul that people should be single, as if being celibate were a condition for people to please heaven. He was taken to heaven while he was celibate and he learned a lot of things, but he was returned onto earth and could easily marry if he wished. It is not marriage that blemishes the soul. It was from the

physically weak mind of Paul that proceeded his desire for people to remain unmarried like him. Could it ever be possible that, I, the Ancient of Days would change if people should follow Paul's counsel and reject marriage, while I decreed that humans should increase, multiply and fill the earth? **Genesis 1:27-29.**

5. I am explaining this clearly because, the enemy is using Paul's teachings to forcefully prevent the leadership of some churches and their membership from getting married. There are many churches on earth whose members are no longer paying attention to the rightful order of marriage, because the enemy has deceived their young men that, remaining celibate amounts to being holy unto the Lord. This made a lot of people consider marriage as an institution that does not favour the believer for the perfection of his holiness. This type of perception does not come from God. I caused it to be written that, being married is better than staying single. **Proverbs 18:22.** Look! This false priesthood abounds in the world with their doctrines based on Paul's teachings, as he stated that the unmarried could give better attention to

the worship of God than the married. **I Corinthians 7:32-34.** I, Jehovah created the woman and brought her to the man in the Garden of Eden. Humans who are the hand's creation of I, Jehovah cannot teach I, their creator in any way. They perceive womanhood unholy and would therefore not make themselves unholy with women, the reason for which they refuse to get married.

6. Their carnal desires render them captives to unnatural practices. When a priest copulates with a colleague priest, it is taken to be holy unto God since it involves no woman. What! Surely have they become prisoners for Satan. **2 Corinthians 6:9-11.** It should be clear to them that, the church has no hope if it has priests that are involved in the sacrilege of copulating with each other. If they believe that womanhood is the source of impurity, then they should have it clear that, all of them who have been born by women have the impurity inherent in them through their delivery. I the creator declare to you that; it does occur that fluid enters the mouth of an infant during delivery and could even get into the stomach. There are times when fluid enters the nostrils, at which times the

need arises that the assigned angels of I, Jehovah should get involved to save the baby. Impurity does not reside in womanhood. Paul, who wrote this was born by a woman, and he has ever been touched by everything about womanhood. I **Corinthians 11:12**.

7. I, Jehovah created woman for Adam and he slept with her to maintain human generation. Which of the priests of this corrupt generation considers himself purer than Adam in the eyes of I, Jehovah? Look! The people who are holy unto I Jehovah are these: Abraham and his wife. Isaac and his wife and Jacob who also had wives. Look! I am the God of the living. **Mark 12:26-27.** What is baffling this present twisted generation is the proverb recording in the book of Revelation. **Revelation 14:4-5.** The lack of understanding of this parabolic phrase which states: "They have not defiled themselves with women, has made many to think that, abstaining from having sexual intimacy with women amounts to purity. This erroneous understanding is the reason behind many people have discarded female companionships and the

devil thus leads them astray and therefore preventing sacred marriages.

8. The blessed promise given Abraham by God was that, his generation will be as numerous as stars. But if he chooses to remain unmarried, how will the promise be fulfilled? **Genesis 17:1-8.** How can a generation be created for a bachelor nation? If all people will comply with Paul's teaching which bases purity on remaining celibate, then reproduction will be stalled in God's nation. In reality, the promise I gave Abraham, Isaac and Jacob, was not given to Paul, but I allowed him to testify about the promised blessings of these married people. **Romans 4:17-25.** You will observe that these promised blessings offered by I, Jehovah cannot match with staying single. It was the gracious mercy offered by the position attained by Abraham in heavenly glory that sanctioned Paul's selection. Therefore, Abraham, whose wife Sarah was had more portion and glory in the sight of heaven than Paul. Paul was not one of the people God had promised, but was only saved by the grace received by those who had the promise. He

therefore came and only became a believer of the things he heard.

9. I had already given the covenant of my promise to inheritors, long before Paul was called into the glory of its grace. It is by grace that believers are drawn to be incorporated into the fold of those who are called, and who own the promise for inheritance. **Hebrews 6:13-20.** Get it clearly that, there exist the fold of the receivers of the promise and there also exist those who are called through the grace for the inheritance of the promised blessing – It is by grace we are saved. **Romans 1:1-7.** Paul's divine call caused Satan to wage war against him in many aspects, just to get him killed. **2 Corinthians 11:22-27.** It is not against Paul alone that Satan wages wars of this sort. Look! He wages war against all faithful prophets and it is the very thing he is doing against you also. However, the life of humans is not in the hands of Satan for him to destroy at will. I Jehovah am the arbiter. Know it, that, Satan had firmly purposed that whoever shall believe in these mysteries and apply them as his order of worship, he will wage a war against him.

10. He also decided that he will fight anybody who will receive these mysteries and apply them to teach any person or church or even the person's own household. If Satan should purpose to scatter people because of these truthful mysteries, look, heaven will also not sit quietly and allow him easily. Study the periods from the beginning of things up till now and see which faithful prophets or believers have I, Jehovah abandoned into the hands of the enemy? Be watchful. **I Peter 5:6-9.** The testimony of the scripture is real, that, your forebears met a lot of afflictions. Satan decided that, any person, who will read this revelation and will take it for a mere trifle and abandon it and speak sacrilege about it as well as about you yourself, such a one shall be considered an important servant in his mission, who shall be heavily rewarded and shall never see any troubles.

11. After Satan realized, he will not be able to kill Paul, he planned to frustrate his divine mission given him from heaven, especially, his teachings. The Holy Spirit revealed this through Peter, as a weakness in Paul and therefore advised all churches and colleague believers to be careful

about Paul's teachings, so that they do not be led astray. **2 Peter 3:13-16.** Paul himself never realized that Satan had invaded some of his teachings. For instance, his visit to the third heaven offered him the power which is the confirmation of the new covenant which he proclaims. Concerning marriage, he received commandment from the Lord, that, a man should not divorce his wife. **I Corinthians 7:10-11.** Moses commanded the people of his time to provide a divorce order and put her off. Satan takes much pleasure in the divorce suit. So when a new commandment was given in place of the divorce order, he was taken by surprise, and thus took a brief thought and drew closer to Paul in his mind. So, after he had pronounced the Lord's order, he went ahead and said; for the rest of the people, it is not the Lord who is telling them. **I Corinthians 7:12.**

12. You will notice that, the second part of Paul's order mentioned the unbeliever and continued that "the one who believes can freely put her off". **I Corinthians 7:15-17.** The question here is that; do God's commandments exist for believers only? Then which God created the unbelievers if the world? I Jehovah am the God of all flesh and do not

belong to a particular fold of humans. **Numbers 21:14-20.** The spirit which led the nation astray and made them dishonor me came on Paul and he spoke as if that was what I had set up for churches. Which part of the law did he give to unbelievers? He stated that, he had received the first order from the Lord that, no one should put off his spouse. This is the commandment of marriage, which offers everlasting life and which proceeds from the spirit of light. It is ordered that, all things should be done in the Lord, and it involves marriage as well. **I Corinthians 7:39-40.**

13. Notice the spirit which spoke through Paul and realize that he has been made captured by Satan. Paul had the courage to advise that I, Jehovah will bless a maiden who will refuse to marry and remain single than another who will marry. **I Corinthians 7:40.** From where did he receive the message and who have I, Jehovah ever called and blessed with celibacy and barrenness? Was it the spirit of I, Jehovah which ordered him to say that, she shall be blessed according to his own mind and no more according to what heaven thinks? I challenge you to select a maiden among you and bless her with

Paul's mind's conception thus; "in the words of Paul, we want you to remain celibate and unproductive, so that you will be barren for ever and ever"; and see if the maiden will consider your statement as a blessing! It was the same evil spirit which caught the mind of Peter, for which Jesus immediately called him "Satan" and cast him away from himself. **Matthew 16:21-23.** Satan sometimes urged Paul to set his mind out as a commandment on behalf of heaven. In the case of King Saul, after he trod the path of his corrupt mind, he fell into Satan's destruction.

14. When Peter advised Jesus with his mind's conception, He called him Satan. What then should Paul be called after he descended from the Mount of congregation and started applying his mind into God's order? Think about it then, that if the message does not proceed from the truth of the Lord of Light, from which master does it come? If it exists according to Paul's mind that the celibate and the barren shall receive more blessing from heaven, then go along and search for the heaven which institutes laws for celibacy and barrenness. But, I, Jehovah, I do not change. I gave the promise

that, one who is barren in the Lord shall have many children. It is not right in the consideration of I, Jehovah that one should remain barren. **Isaiah 54:1-6, Isaiah 65:21-24.** You, barren, who have never brought forth, extend your tent. Look! I am uncovering all these for you, who are hearing my messages and writing them that, you should be alert so that the devil that causes prophets to act differently does not cause you, Victor to lead the nation astray by instituting orders for them with some of the conceptions of your mind. Verily do I declare to you that, if you submit yourself unto the devil and receive his counsel to institute orders for the church, the congregation will stray away from the Lord of Light and the master of the physical mind's conceptions will take over its place.

15. If this happens to you, heaven will withdraw its support and you will be left alone and be conquered in the midst of your enemies. Due to the ensuing issues therefore, be alert with the message and never write what you are not told for the church for it to go astray. This satanic spirit frequently found this fault on Paul for the reason that, he often applied his own mind in addition to

the divine mysteries given him from heaven. Meanwhile, it is he himself who testified that, he was made to know heavenly mysteries by the grace of God. Such testimonies about himself is an indication that, he himself did not know what was going on. **Acts 20:22-33.** Satan, having observed that the nation accepted every pronouncement that proceeded out of his mouth as having been spoken by God, he tried to always impose its spirit onto Paul's mind. If Paul had stated the order of marriage in the straight forward manner he received it from the Lord, the excessive straying taking place in the churches today would have been curtailed. After the Lord himself spoke about the order of marriage, he added no more. **Matthew 19:1-11.**

16. After Peter heard the laws of marriage, he lamented, saying, if it be so between spouses, then there is no need to marry. This lamentation went through all generations, and for that matter, when a different law came through Paul that, spouses could be put off as a result of unbelief, many people embraced this weak teaching and so, they divorce their spouses and marry new ones freely.

The Lord of the spirit of Light does not sanction divorce. There is no middle stand or no other way as far as this is concerned. Believers are not taking delight in complying with the laws and orders of the narrow gate. This is the reason, if any prophet of God should change the law, it draws the whole church into waywardness.

17. Paul taught and warned that stuttering tongue is not entertained in the presence of God. I called Moses to be used as a bearer of my messages but he gave the excuse that, he was a stammerer. It was after I chose his brother Aaron that my words begun to proceed and just as I was in the beginning so do I remain. It was Paul who gave the law. **2 Corinthians 14:21-22.** It is clear according to the law that, that which belongs to the believer is prophecy. If he had stopped here, the excessive application of unintelligible tongues in churches would not have advanced so far. He however went ahead and said, interpreters should be sought; for what? If something is needless to the believer, then it should not even be mentioned in the midst of believers. Since Paul did not fully emphasize it; the weak aspect became attractive to most Christian

churches of today to be chosen for application, to which they are firmly attached. This is the reason they all compulsorily demonstrate the sign of lunacy in all their gatherings. That which is weak is close to corruption and is good for nothing. **I Corinthians 14:18-19.**

18. Churches must be aware that Paul made a lot of statements, many of which have been taken as orders or worship in these end times, but it is not all of them that proceeded from the teachings of heaven and it is not all which have been approved by heaven. The churches should therefore seek the confirmation of these statements from I, Jehovah prior to accepting them as their doctrines. I am Jehovah and I do not change my pronouncements. I do not use the stuttering tongue for anything. **Ezekiel 13:1-6.** Since Paul wrote it and they all come to love the stuttering tongue, they got captured by the false spirit, for which reason they got abandoned by heaven to practice it according to the inordinate desires of their hearts. What the scripture records against stuttering tongue will effectively manifest upon them. How could people think that I, Jehovah have become God of

stuttering tongue? Due to stuttering tongues, they bleat and hiss in the chapels like senseless beasts. They will so remain because even if heaven sends them warnings, they will not change their minds unless they have the manifestation. **Isaiah 23:9-13.**

19. When the order of the Holy Communion was revealed to Paul, he taught the corrective measures strictly without any addition of his own mind's conceptions, an indication that what was revealed to him in vision was the very thing recorded in the scripture and heaven approved of it. He indicated elsewhere in his teachings that the master of sin was in him since it was revealed to him through the spirit of the truth. **Romans 7:20-25.** The meaning of this is that, Paul matched the state of his spiritual being with the actions of his physical self. So people who do not fully understand spiritual things get weakened and depend on that statement to claim being ordered by Satan to commit the sins for which they are apprehended, for they themselves are unaware of what they had done and could therefore not be responsible for them. Another commandment Paul declared to be at war in his mind is true. This is the warfare from the devil,

which forced him to falter in the gospel he proclaimed. If you, also do not remain alert, this sickness of the mind will put many of you in trouble.

20. If a suspect is arraigned in court for an alleged offence and he applies Paul's statement in his defense that an agent of the crime, hidden in him committed it, and not him personally, do you believe the court will agree that it is the agent of the crime in the man which is at fault, and not the man himself and will therefore acquit the suspect? Who among you will accept the excuse of a young man who defiles his or her daughter, claiming that, it was the spirit of fornication which is in him that committed the defilement and not he as an individual so he should be acquitted? What do you think about heavenly trials if the unrighteous judges on earth will not let go such persons? You therefore have to be careful about Paul's teachings; and not Paul's alone but also all prophets. This is because no one born of a woman is without fault; know therefore that every prophet has some physical weakness.

21. It is for the correction of such things that the commandment of heaven is recorded in the scripture, so that the Comforter does not speak on his own, but should rather take it from what has already been recorded so that, in case some corrections are required, they should be done by the spirit. **John 16:12-14.** When I said, you Victor ought to be spoken to by the Other Comforter, do you think it was to be an easy experience before He speaks to you? Look! The troubles inherent in such things are not well known to humans, so have the troubles you are going through taken you unawares. Some of your colleagues have even thought that it was your weakness and your sins that brought the problems; for which many people pray that, God should uncover your stealthy deeds. Look! I am the Ancient of Days! Have I ever been defeated by the creation of something? If there exist any obscurity, will it defeat the sight of I, Jehovah, within the person? **Psalms 33:12-15.** I have observed it from my glorious abode that you are attempting to accept this type of fault and weakness onto yourself, and have therefore become anxious because of the occurrence of

certain mishaps for which you are no longer able to do your writing.

22. Get if clearly that, it is not for any faults that the devil is waging war against you, for this is what he always does against the specially selected saints; including you. **Psalms 59:2-6.** Your plight was examined in heaven with the testimony of this scripture and the need arose for you to be strengthened by explaining the messages to you. Whatever attempts the enemy makes, the order has already been given that the Other Comforter speaks to you. Though the enemy fought seriously with Paul, he could not defeat him. I mentioned these for the affirmation of your faith, so you don't tremble and get confused. Verily truly, had it not been the Other Comforter who used to come and speak with Paul, to guide him in many instances, Satan would have killed him for long and the gospel would not have grown for people to hear. It is not Paul's faults that caused his persecution and threat of death; and it is not your faults as Victor, for which you are being threatened with death. The truth is that, all ordained prophets and priests are anchored by the spirit of God's grace from heaven

with the law and order of the teachings, to be applied to guide God's nation to heaven.

23. If the ordained is attached to heaven and never strayed and is therefore blessed with his church by divine glory, then the enemy wages war against them fiercely. The grace bestowed on you Victor also, to be spoken to by the forefront spirits of heaven will not let the enemy sit idle. These were the things the Other Comforter explained to Paul, for which he considered all his troubles as a pleasure, because he came to understand that, it was as a result of the mysteries sent through him that the enemy is at war, and so it is for you Victor also. **Colossians 1:24-29.** When the fights Paul fought are revealed to you, your heart will be affirmed and your faith will not tremble. When Satan realized, Paul was taken to the third heavens, he firmly planned to kill him. He knew very well that his soul would not belong to him, if he was killed; and really it was not for his soul that he wanted him killed, but his opposition to the gospel, because the receiver of mystery uses his mind and mouth for its proclamation. Satan therefore desires

the death of such people so that they do not live and continue to proclaim the gospel.

Chapter 6.

The Other Comforter was the power of the Holy Spirit which guided Paul to accomplish his mission.

1. Heaven, having observed that it was because of Paul's endowment with mysteries that Satan waged war against him, sent the Other Comforter to guide him. Due to the same reason, the Other Comforter has to be sent to you Victor also to guide you. I bring these examples to see how the Other Comforter defended Paul's life. After Satan struck him and his church with the present-day pleasure of adultery, they got scattered and left him alone. **2 Timothy 4:9-11.** Satan always desired in like manner to scatter people from the receiver of mysteries, so he will remain alone and become an easy prey for him. However, if the mystery bearer has prayer supporters who pray fervently, Satan

gets frustrated in the war. After applying the cunning scheme to scatter people from Paul, he faced him squarely and had it not been the support of the Other Comforter, he would have been defeated. This is the reason Paul never depended on men. **2 Timothy 4:16-18.** What Paul should have known is that his deliverance was not in the efforts of men but from heaven rather.

2. You also have to take note of these, so as to be alert in order not to put your hope on human beings. **Psalms 118:7-9.** After Satan exhausted him efforts and could do no more, he decided to betray him to the power of earthly kingdoms so that he would be arrested, tried and be given the death penalty. However, the more Satan tried to threaten his life, the more heaven increased his years. Satan employed a lot of schemes to cut short his life, but he was always saved by the Other Comforter; and so, it is for you also today. **2 Corinthians 11:23-33.** I want you to read these things into which Satan pushed Paul with the intention of killing him, but with his knowledge of the Other Comforter's

support, he had courage and went through them all. My advice to you, should any of these things happen to you is to pluck enough courage since the Other Comforter is at your disposal. **I John 2:1-3.**

3. That which greatly pleases the Other Comforter is for people to adhere strictly to his instructions and comply accordingly. These are the people who fellowship with Him and He will never forsake them into the hands of the enemy. You need to obey this Comforter closely and hold fast to his instructions so that he will provide you with light and victory. When Paul held onto his instructions, he strengthened him and he went ahead and proclaimed the gospel in all places. The Holy Spirit revealed it to Christ that He will be arrested if He went to Jerusalem, but He went, knowing it well, because of the gospel. **Matthew 16:21-24.** It was this same spirit which encouraged Paul, while in good knowledge that, he would be arrested if he went to Jerusalem, but he did go, because of the gospel. **Acts 21:1-6, 21:8-14.** Any time he visited the brethren, there always were prophecies to test him to see if he would be afraid and refuse to forge

ahead with the mission. Had he not been strengthened by the Other Comforter, he would, as a human being have been afraid of death and refuse to go to Jerusalem. Heaven knows he ought to go to Jerusalem and proclaim the mystery over there and not to go there to die.

4. In a state of confusion and fear, he had pity for some brethren and wanted to stay with them in peace, When the Lord gave him a prophecy, it was not about death. **Acts 18:9-11.** Oftentimes, people dream dreams which discourage them, but since God does not plan misfortune for His own, things seen in dreams do not manifest. I am Jehovah. People had visions that Paul was going to die in Jerusalem, but the reality in the sight of God was that, Paul should live and proclaim the gospel. Apply these examples to strengthen your faiths. Despite the fears expressed by the visioners for him, he had courage from the Other Comforter and bid the church and its leaders' farewell. **Acts 20:17-38.** Paul ought to have set off after the farewell message but he warned them to be alert because the self-conceited and wild wolves would invade the church with the aim to destroy it, but Satan

made it that, they rather grieved about Paul's departure and did not pay much attention to the warning.

5. Look! This is what always happens, that the church always looked upon the leaders and if his days are over and he dies, the ministry is destroyed because of the alertness of human beings. Do not let this happen to you. I, the Ancient of Days commit you into the hands of the Other Comforter, so remain faithful in these instructions. The enemy drew Paul's faith to depend on humans on his immediate arrival in Jerusalem and he accepted their counsel. It was the number of the people who went into the temple with him that struck others to want to know what was happening before they spotted Paul. If he had totally relied on the Other Comforter and went alone into the temple to perform his purification rites, he would not have been given out in a riot. – Be wary of people's advice that incite fears. **Acts 21:15-26.** While caught up in the trap of dependency, Satan relied those who apply God's name in cunningness round him, which caused riot and he was taken a prisoner. **Acts 21:27-33.**

6. Do recollect seriously, that no one ought to exalt himself if he is not fully prepared by the grace for special assignments. When the light of the gospel shone on Paul on his way to Damascus, the spirit did not permit him to proclaim it in Jerusalem because he had not yet received the mystery. By exercising sufficient patience, he finally received the spirit of the mystery which was to allow him to be received easily in Jerusalem. The riot that ensued did not give him the opportunity to do the proclamation. If rather came that, he should defend himself before the courts, a situation that pleased Satan so much. Satan then wanted to use state authority and imprisonment to stop Paul. Then the Other Comforter changed the minds of the judges immediately because, Romans did not consider Jewish laws as statutes for governance. This made the Jews' accusation of Paul a mere trivia before the Roman laws and their judges. The Other Comforter ensured that Paul was not beaten. **Acts 22:24-30.**

7. It would have been appropriate if the Other Comforter released Paul from prison and led him to go and proclaim the mystery but Satan desired

that, he should be brought before the governors so that he would organize thugs to beat him to death. **Acts 23:12-16.** It was by the deed of the Other Comforter that the presence of Paul's nephew was not noticed by the thugs while he was with them; and He further softened the captain to accept Paul's request. Satan had a different mind from the conspirators he had incited to kill Paul, so confusion ensued. He desired Paul killed to prevent the proclamation of the mystery; but he also knows that using the mystery as a charge was baseless because the people did not know what the mystery was. This is the reason he incited them to kill him for defiling the temples meanwhile Satan has no business to do with the temple. The Other Comforter, having observed that there was no unity of purpose between Satan and the conspirators, he confused them and this confusion resulted into Paul being released briefly, but while he felt discouraged, the Lord revealed Himself to him in a vision. **Acts 23:7-11.**

8. The Other Comforter now used the chief captains in a guise for Paul to proclaim the mystery. He caused him to be protected but under the

consideration as a prisoner. He was taken round a lot, and he himself wanted to be going out in that manner to proclaim the word. The decision of the captain rather benefited him, otherwise there were a lot of places he could not have visited on his own. **Acts 23:20-31.** The Other Comforter made it possible for the captains to agree to send Paul to Rome. Think about the number of soldiers that were sent to guard Paul alone. The only concern was that, death should not cross them on the journey. Even though, humans might impose: death sentence on him, heaven had given him special protection among his killers. Look! I am telling you all this to make you aware that Satan wages war against mystery receivers seriously. He wished to kill Paul because of the mysteries, and you also, it is not for any other reason that you are suffering, but just as a result of the mysteries you are writing. On his trip to Rome, Satan attempted inciting people to kill him on the way. But when they heard that, a great number of soldiers were in guard, they got scared and did not pursue him.

9. Due to his proclamation of the gospel, he was given relief and the captain even ordered that he

should be permitted to give audience to his visitors. **Acts 24:20-23.** Paul spoke through the power of the spirit when he stood before Governor Felix and his wife Felix could have accepted the gospel had he not been filled with the urge to collect bribe. He could not receive the gospel, but he left Paul in prison expecting him to give him some money. **Acts 24:24-27.** The Other Comforter delivered Paul from Felix's court and sent him to a chief captain so he will also hear the gospel. The Holy Spirit allowed Paul to proclaim the gospel to this captain as well. However, Satan wanted to let state authorities find Paul guilty at all cost, but the governors and the captains could not find any instruments on which to charge him and find him guilty. He defended himself before different governors and it did happen that, wherever he defended himself, the gospel was proclaimed. **Acts 25:8-12.**

10. The Holy Spirit, in a quest to cause the gospel proclaimed in all places let the Other Comforter to lead Paul to other captains, for the spirit wanted to use state authorities and captains as a platform for the proclamation of the mystery to the whole world. For this reason, anywhere Paul was sent to,

be it a prison, or in the courts of state authorities or before army captains, the Other Comforter was always with him and delivered him from all his enemies. In Ephesus, their goddess Diana was so much precious to them and they believed it fell from heaven, so Satan made them revere it so much without joke. Paul's gospel message captivated Diana and its priests; they therefore conspired to kill him but the Other Comforter saved him from their plan. **Acts 19:33-41.** In reality, the Other Comforter has come to help you and teach you the whole truth. It is therefore important that, all his messages be written down for you, so that you will be reading them and apply them to remind yourselves. Be aware that, the enemy knows that, when people read the books, they will understand and adhere to the messages and conquer him by complying with them, so does he make people lazy, not to read the books.

11. After Paul realized in his time that the churches were not enthusiastic with reading the books, he warned and vowed to them in the name of Jesus to read the books in all the congregations. **Colossians 4:10-18.** Though Paul used to encourage the

churches fervently, the enemy was able to draw his colleague Demas and some of his beloved fellows away. Demas was identified in the salutation addressed to the Colossian Church as a steadfast colleague, but when they arrived in Thessalonica, Demas abandoned the holy congregation and turned to the pleasures of the present world. **2 Timothy 4:9-10.** Now, then, you have to be alert with serious prayers, particularly for the leaders among you. This is because it is very easy for Satan to lead many people astray in the present crisis world, just as he did it in Paul's time. Remember the advice of our Lord Jesus Christ that, one should agree to lose a lot of things for the sake of the heavenly kingdom. **Matthew 19:28-30.** Demas and some other colleagues appeared as if they were fore runners of the believers but the spirit of the present world deluded him and he left for Thessalonica where the man of sin reveals himself as God, whereas he is nothing but deception. **2 Thessalonians 2:3-5.**

12. Learn this from Paul's faith that, when they were in the boat and it was about to drown, he advised that their belongings should be thrown into

the sea to make the boat lighter. It wasn't the items were thrown into the sea, to be retrieved after the storm, but that, they be lost forever but their lives be saved. **Acts 27:18-25.** After throwing off their things they all got into fasting prayers, committing their lives into the hands of God, for there was no signal of hope for life. At the time all hope was lost and no one knew where salvage was to come from, it was that same night that Paul had a revelation, and when he believed it, especially that, not a strand of hair of any one of them was going to get lost, they had courage, and deliverance came in a miraculous way through the revelation. You also have to know that the church you are in today is just like a boat which secures the lives of its occupants, and that the crises of this world could make a believer lose his precious things because of the faith.

13. There are certain temptations which severity could make a believer declare that, better would it be, if he had not been born into the world. Look! I, still declare to you that, you need enough long suffering to be able to remain in the faith. **Job 10:32-36.** The church you are in is in the middle of

life's tempest. Use faith, fasting prayer and long suffering as your sail and its support for your life's boat, so you will not get drawn or experience a wreck. Satan will raid your belongings, be it through jealous relatives and others. Learn long suffering and defend not your righteousness. Your precious things could be raided and they would be captured by thieves and robbers, therefore learn to exercise restraint in all that you will lose because of your faith. It behooves spouses to learn long-suffering. Husbands and wives could experience cheating each from the other. **I Corinthians 6:7-8.** Learn it from me about the raid your things suffer, that nature has not endowed humans to stand aloof when precious things are being raided without making any efforts of defense. There is not a single person like that. However, one who cannot withstand such a temptation cannot please God.

14.   There are several divine doctrines, which practice cannot be done by humans on their own unless they are given power from the spirit in which the laws are accomplished in heaven. I testify to you that the commandments of the heavenly kingdom have been accomplished in the

Other Comforter. He will strengthen you to remain steadfast in the faith. The strengthening instructions of this spirit are many, the reason for which they should be written down for you for remembrance. Just as the spirit guided Paul during his days of proclaiming the gospel, so will He guide all who display enthusiasm amongst you. **Titus 2:11-15.** This spirit revealed itself to Paul frequently, so he always had courage. The enemy attempted leading Paul astray through chief captains and state authorities with the intention of finding fault with him so they would dwell upon that and kill him. After the spirit delivered him from Governor Felix, Satan caused his betrayal into the hands of King Agrippa and Bernice but the king favoured his case and did not deliver him to the conspirators as they requested. While he was with King Agrippa, the conspirators thought he was going to deliver him to them to be killed. **Acts 26:27-32.**

15. The great surprise the conspirators met in Agrippa's court was his declaration that, Paul's words nearly converted him into Christianity. They lost hope here again. I declare to you that, it was

the Other Comforter who saved Paul from all the accusations, but since the conspirators were ignorant of this, they thought that Paul will by all means be convicted for execution if the case was presented to a different governor. Satan then came to realize that, the more he caused Paul to be sent from one court to the other, the more he had the opportunity to proclaim the revelation of Christ, and he was not convicted at any of the courts. What annoyed him the more was how he was not being treated as other prisoners were being treated but he was always given freedom and relief. **Acts 27:1-3.** It was not in any case the mind of the captains to give him solace during his prison terms but rather the power of the Other Comforter did it. You will also observe that, Satan had incited some of the guards to kill all the prisoners at the time they experienced the shipwreck, so that none of them would escape. The Other Comforter saved all of them because of Paul. **Acts 27:39-44.**

16. The trip to Rome was long and the frightening experience of traveling on the ocean made them consider all the occupants of the boat as prisoners. All this while, the guards taking Paul along knew

almost nothing about him. All other prisoners were arrested for some wrong doing but Paul was there for no wrong doing. For this reason, when the boat sailed ashore in a coastal city, the spirit allowed him to proclaim the gospel and he healed people. **Acts 28:7-10.** From this time, after the captain and the guard team noticed that he was a gospel proclamant, they began to consider him a special person. On their arrival in Rome, the captain ordered that, he should be taken to the fellow believers. **Acts 28:16-20.** Consider the occurring myth of how it happened that Paul was granted the freedom, to the extent that, all his guards rather turned to become his armour bearers who took him round to proclaim the gospel. **Acts 28:30-31.** Satan came to realize after all this while, that the attempt to stop the gospel was not going to be successful.

17. He also realized that, for a state authority to accuse and convict Paul, he must be seen to have contravened some state laws. The came a wicked governor to Rome at the time, who decided to review all trials and understand their various terms of conviction. When he reviewed Paul's case, he

realized that he had no terms of conviction. It was this governor who sought after Paul and committed him to trial on the charge that, he escaped from jail. When he was brought for trial, he had grown to become a fairly old man, and he was convicted with a young soldier. The soldier was killed because of Paul and Paul himself was beheaded. But the fact remains that Paul never escaped from jail.

18. Paul was convicted under the Roman law of escaping from prison and was beheaded and a soldier was killed because of him. The question is that; where was the Other Comforter, to be unable to save him as he had done for him on several previous occasions? Very truly, I declare to you that this Other Comforter was with him and it was He who reduced his pain so that his soul could get to the position of reward attained by the foremost souls. **Revelation 20:4-6.** Victor, I declare to you. This position will befit you also. Look! The understanding of these things is difficult for the human mind. It is the special responsibility of the Other Comforter to mitigate the excessive pain of the flesh, so the humans can pass through into everlasting sleep. I am affirming to you that; some

selected saints have already attained this position. **Revelation 6:9-11.** The scripture made reference to some colleagues who are in the world, who deserve to come and meet the forebears, to attain the required number. Paul has completed his fight. **2 Timothy 4:7-8.** This glorious position is waiting in spirit, the reason for which you ought to be assisted so that, these messages so recorded be made manifest. **Daniel 11:33-36.** I rest my words of encouragement here. Let the Other Comforter bring you all home in the spirit. Amen! **I Peter 5:10-11.**

GOD'S SPIRIT OF JUDGEMENT.

Chapter 1.

Serious deception will commit many worshippers into judgement. The revelation of prophecy will uncover the deception for believers and deliver them into eternity.

1. In the night of 7th February 1997, I, Victor Nyarko Amoah had a dream in which I saw that the whole world was in a great riot, the atmosphere was hazy and the skies laden with clouds, threatening a torrential rain. I saw a sign in the skies in the form of a huge dragon flying. It was throwing some materials in the form of pieces of paper onto the ground. I noticed that anybody who picked the piece of material immediately bowed and begun to speak in various unintelligible languages. I fixed my eyes into the skies and saw a

figure in the semblance of an angel; also flying, lower than the dragon, so that, if one does not watch carefully, one may not see the dragon, except the angel. The angel had a trumpet, with which he announced that: This is the almighty; woe unto anybody who will not bow to him. **Revelation 13:15.**

2. After hearing the announcement and looking once again at the dragon, I immediately realized that, it was not an angel of the Lord Almighty. Since the dragon was far above in the sky than the angel, people were not able to see it. People therefore thought this angel was one of the Holy Spirit. It therefore deceived many people to bow to it. **Revelation 13:7-8.** Since I realized that I ought not bow to this angel of dragon, I decided to hide myself. Since this angel was far above in the sky, it was watching almost all places. I started running away from it and suddenly I arrived at the sea

shore. I presently heard a loud noise in the sky and tuned to see what it was, then the dragon appeared suddenly in a fierce speed in an attempt to pick me up in the manner that a hawk preys on a chicken. I quickly laid on the ground and it missed me and went and feel deep into the see. The sea suffered a great tempest with a dreadful noise.

3. With great fear, I took a flight back to the town and heard people still praising the angle at the top of their voices thus: "Who can withstand his kingdom?" **Revelation   13:4.** Then surfaced an apparition on the clouds in confirmation of what Jesus said about His second coming. It brightened from the west toward the east. **Matthew 24:25-28.** Recall what Jesus said about great signs appearing on the skies to signify his second coming. **Luke 21:25-28.** There appeared a huge rainbow stretch from the east to the west. The brightness of this rainbow caused the angel to fall into the sea,

causing all to make a fearful noise. I heard a voice at the back of the rainbow proclaiming that: "The kingdom is at hand and the end of all is near". The voice continued that: Blessed are those who will persevere in righteousness during the afflicting period of this rainbow cloud, "for it must remain on the cloud for six long months; and only the one who will overcome shall enter everlasting life".

4. I also saw that the rainbow caused rain not to fall on earth for a whole six months and there was no night. Then came a voice saying; the signs of the coming of the Lamb are in two parts. These are the signs of labour and delivery and that, they shall be blessed, those who the Lamb shall reveal the delivery sign to. The rainbow is demonstrating the signs of the delivery. After this voice ceased, many people said it was a thunder's blow. This however signifies that; saintly prophets understand the import of thunders but ordinary people would

consider it a mere thunder. The rainbow caused a rise in atmospheric temperation, resulting in a heat wave which brought a lot of sicknesses including painful boils. As a result of the affliction caused by the rainbow, all nations of the world called a conference to deliberate on what to do to destroy the rainbow, so it will cease to afflict the earth. Mighty missiles were shot into the skies but the shots could not get near the rainbow. The effect of the missiles rather resulted into dreadful diseases on the earth.

5. The severity of the afflictions resulted into famine and some parents even smashed the heads of their children, for having become burdens to them. The afflictions were so fierce that, some people even cursed the Most High. **Revelation 16:9.** Then arrived a man from hades, who deceived people that he has been sent by God to save humans from the rainbow's afflictions.

Revelation 9:10-11. He called himself the prince of peace and ordered that 666 people should be sealed for God in the world so that the rainbow would   disappear. All the kings of the world welcomed his counsel and the seal was made on people in towns and villages all over. All who refused to be sealed were imprisoned for being enemies of peace and they were tortured till they all died. The torture included cutting their fingers one after the other and were to answer whether they want peace or were in support of the rainbow. All who supported the rainbow were torture to death in prison. **Revelation 13:9-10.**

6. All nations of the world stopped warring against each other and went with one mind to fight the rainbow. In the melee of this strife arrived two prophets of the Holy Spirit who proclaimed that: "anyone who does not receive the sign of the Jesus

Christ, who rose from the dead shall go to hell". They made the proclamation with courage, asking people to praise the rainbow and its afflictions and revere God. This proclamation enraged Satan and his warriors so much that they incited the world leaders against them, to arrest and kill them. **Revelation 11:6-8.** Three days after they were killed, they resurrected with some saints and went back to heaven. After they had gone to heaven, the rainbow disappeared. Then the antichrist and the angel of hades deceived the people that, it was the murder of the two prophets that cause the wrath of God to cease, for they caused the afflictions to the world and people believed them.

7. Three days after the rise of the saints to heaven, a torrential rain fell with heavy snow blocks, which hit many people to death. Their blood flowed into rivers and the rivers turned into blood and the rivers that flowed into the ocean caused it also to

turn into blood. Then begun the descent of the Holy City onto earth after the torrential rain. Be watchful therefore, for, there shall come many deceptive agents, who shall proclaim that, it is on this day or the other that He shall come. Do not believe them, for it is the whole kingdom which is going to descend and this is not going to be a single day's sign. From the days of the sign of labour to the sign of delivery; it cannot be a matter of a day. Look! It is the rainbow which signifies the seal of the affliction and it is during these days that shall the kingdom descend, and then, after a thousand years, judgement shall be established. **Numbers 24:14-19.**

8. Look! I want to make it clear to you, Victor that many who have become teachers in the church are unable to understand the spiritual charges you are receiving for the leadership of the church. This is because they all have become priest and want to

be so considered. Even though the Lord Jesus Christ was ordained in the priestly order of Melchizedek, He worked in the spirit of prophecy. **Hebrews 5:4-10.** It is the enemy that causes a great position of reverence for priests, but Jehovah God reserves greater reverence for true prophets and in fact God and His angels have more courage in prophets rather than trusting in priests. Though the Lord Jesus Christ was ordained priest in heaven and on earth, he did not perform the salvation assignment in the spirit of priesthood but He rather abided in the spirit of prophecy which led Elijah. **Revelation 19:9-10.** Victor, warn your compatriots who think within themselves that they are priests that they are separating themselves from the spirit of Jesus. It the Lord Jesus has abided in the spirit of priesthood whole on earth, he would have been drawn into the same faults found on the priests of the world.

9. If you people, who are not as firm as the Lord Jesus would think you would abandon the spirit of prophecy and its revelation and apply the spirit of priesthood to lead the flock, you will be fed up and conquered for having forsaken the spirit of Jesus. Look for the meaning of this scripture in order to unearth realization. **I Peter 4:17-19.** Acknowledge this fact that, it is better abiding in the spirit of prophecy than in the spirit of priesthood. Jesus cried to the father with tears in prayer for the sins of the nations, but what testimony had Aaron that he offered the father anything for the life of the nation? If he did not receive anything from the nation, he could not offer a sacrifice. Yet, the things he collected from the nation called into God's memory, the nation's sins. **Hebrews 10:3-10.** Look! You do not understand what the scripture says that, He had removed the first thing in order to establish the second. The self-conceited on their path never consult God, but rather do everything on their own.

10. Satan gets easy hold of such people and if he throws them aground due to their hardheartedness and stupidity, they tend to blame heaven, claiming that God did not lend them support. If you do remain alert in all you do and do them according to the second order of the Lord and not in the old one, God will not put you to shame. The first covenant receives items from the nation for sacrifices, but in the second covenant, the priest sacrifices himself and his time without receiving anything because Christ also did not receive anything from the nation, but gave out himself. **Hebrews 9:11-12.**

11. Just as Jesus sacrificed himself, so does it behoove you leaders of the Lamb to learn to sacrifice yourselves. Look! I am the Angel of Judgement. Very truly, I tell you, Jehovah God shall judge His nation. **Hebrews 10:30-31.** The Angel of

Judgment has been sent to correct you, so that you are not judged together with the world. It is however not many of the churches of the world that will receive the prophecy of this angel before the day of judgement comes. Blessed are those who will hear the voice of this angel today and repent. They shall be saved by the Lord. **Hebrews 3:7-14.** The power of the grace that saves is in the commandment. It is not by the work of the law that people are vindicated, but in the absence of the law, no one can draw near the family of God, but would be forsaken by the grace. Jesus the Lord gave us, angels the law so that we shall draw close to those who have turned to the order established by Christ. **Galatians 3:19-20.**

12. This scripture signifies that, many are those who received the grace for priesthood or the service of sacrifice, but it does not follow that just as people are numerous, so should everybody lead

the church of Christ with his mind's conception. Look! You are sufficient with grace and God is only one. If you are as numerous as the sand on the beach and you all receive the order from the one God, you will be united in voice and the enemy can never defeat you. Endeavour to perform your salvation duty with self-sacrifice. **Galatians 6:1-5.** Do recall that it is written in your judgement book that, remember to ensure that one who is taught in word should fellowship with his master in the performance of all good work. **Galatians 6:6-10.** Recall that just as Jesus the Lord rebuked the scribes to receive the law according to the power of angels and they refused, so is it going on in the present day. The Angel of Judgement wants to ensure that you are reminded about the commandments and you comply with them perfectly more than the ancient people.

13. The children of today will harden their hearts and will not repent because they act according to the first thing which the Lord Jesus came to remove, and are therefore at a loss with themselves and the temptations of their congregations. Remember that before the real end comes, heavenly angels will come and separate the righteous from the sinful men. **Matthew 13:47-50.** Look! Victor, take it that, before I separate righteous men from sinful ones, the law ought to be read to them once again in order to differentiate between the obedient and the disobedient. If you were found in good fellowship with the spirit of prophecy sent to your church, you would have been free from judgement. When the Lord first revealed Himself and you received His messages, you did not take good care of them afterwards. **John 14:21.** When Michael, the Leader of your compatriots appeared to the church, you confused his messages with doubt and wanton

criticism, so you do not have a mastery of His words for leading the church. **Daniel 12:1.**

14. When the Comforter came, you altered His words and He nearly fought with you because of your hard heartedness. **Isaiah 63:8-10.** Look! When Jesus, the Lord probed the work of the scribes and the Pharisees, He observed they were wayward, but they considered themselves righteous. **Matthew 5:20.** It is pathetic for one to consider himself great and righteous, whereas in the consideration of God, he should be a worthless person without any hope for everlasting life. **Colossians 2:18-19.** Behold! Do not ensemble such vicious leaders. Complacency and self-aggrandizement have caused the devil to invade the church and has established a place for his cohorts. This is the reason sicknesses and crises are on the increase amongst you. Satan has coached a lot of people, to the extent that they have become

his representatives in the church. Such people hold brief for Lucifer. Representatives of Lucifer abound in all gathering in order to suppress the righteous with the objective to collapse the church. Satan has also coached some on how to remain in the spirit of Herod. **Matthew 2:6-8.** Such people have an outward look as enthusiasts in the worship of God but in their hearts is cunningness. They speak peacefully with their fellows but harbour evil in their minds. **Psalms 140:7-12.**

15. Ensures settlements amongst you first and foremost so that the Lord will hasten when you pray to fight with the wicked nation and deliver you from the cunning man. There abound enemies in eliqque of men and women in the church. Since the hearts of such schemers are filled with wiles, they are able to sacrifice their children or even themselves to ensure the devil demonstrates its victory so that the church be overcome with fear.

Some of them even agree to die, to serve as a treacherous example to discredit the church of Christ. Due to this therefore, you Victor, listen attentively. If you are praying for a sick person, whose spirit has no blemish before the Lord, his healing comes quickly. If the healing however retards, then you must know there is something against the person. Never lose hope, however continue with the prayers, but set him aside, so that his weakness is not used to drive others away from the faith. Take heart and pluck courage, so you will overcome.

16. Victor, I have not observed your effort to be yet enough for forging ahead in the faith. This is because, you have not been observed to equal your forebears in their testimony of faith as indicated in the scriptures. **I. Thessalonians 1:4-7.** Very truly I tell you; if you exercise patience, you will come to identify those chosen by the Lord Jesus for Himself.

Their obedience with demonstrate that they are children of everlasting life in the church. Those in the church, who have not been chosen dwell in the spirit of the mystery of iniquity. Their lifestyle is all iniquity but they are hidden, just to baffle many people. It however behooves you to be examples to the present world, so that even if the gospel should be covered, it will progress powerfully amongst you, to the glory and honour of the Father.

17. Now, your fear of sickness and death has rendered you unable to make manifest the prophecy. **Isaiah 8:16-18.** Look! Victor, fear you not; repent and gird the loins of your minds with the testimonies of the Lord, so that you will remain alert in order not to fall into judgement. **I. Peter 1:13-15.** For you to be used as examples, you need to be seen in the faith required by the Lord from believers, for it is this type of faith that pleases the

Lord Jesus. For instance, when the wicked King set a furnace and threw the three young men who refused to bow to his golden idol into it, they were save by the Lord. **Daniel 3:14-19.** When you read these things today, you take them for a trivia or you at times do not give it a thought at all. When these young men agreed to be put into the fire after critically examining it, where then have they agreed to go to? They agreed to die for the sake of Jehovah God. This is where the Lord sent the Angel of Judgement for a selection.

18. I, The Angel of Judgement descended on top of the furnace and I used God's pronouncement prophesied through his prophets to give a verdict. **Isaiah 33:13-16.** The young men were not afraid when they were being taken to the furnace, and neither did a human being or a spirit forewarned them to go because the fire was not going to consume them. Look! The faith of the young men,

which made them agree to die drew down the power of God. And this is the voice of the Angel of Judgement. "Who can dwell with burning embers and who can abide with Jehovah, the consuming fire?" Had the Angel of Judgement found anything evil on the young men, the fire would have burned them. They were delivered because they had the Lord's commandments in their hearts, with which they complied. The men who threw them into the furnace however did not have the Lord's covenant in them, so they were burnt to death by the flames. What then did the scripture say about you children of today? The commandment is in your heart and in your mouth to be complied with. It is not for nothing that the covenant has been given to you but for compliance.

19. As for you, anger and quarrelling have taken the place of the commandment in your hearts, the reason for which the testimonies are not getting

manifest for you. Look, Victor then at Daniel. When he was convicted and given to hungry lions to be consumed, he knows very well that he was going into hungry lions' den, but he agreed to freely died. No one told him he would eventually be delivered from the lions. The lions, having been died feeding signifies a fast and since Daniel was fasting, the Angel of Judgement gave the verdict that, Daniel's life be saved through fasting in fulfillment of the prophecy. **Joel. 2:12-17.** Had Daniel not learnt to fast incessantly, he would have perished. Those who were devoured by the lions knew nothing about the Lord's commandments. The path of the perfect faith is the one recorded in the scripture that: "I will put the law in their mouth and in their mind". **Romans 10:6-9.** The meaning of the phrase, "the law is in your mouth to be complied with", is that, anger, insults and evil thoughts against fellows should have no place at all in you.

20. Take Lot and his household as example. After the Angel of Judgement watched your homes in the church, he observed Satan's arms to be up on you. The total households of Abraham, and Lot, their wives and children were receivers of angel visitors and the angels never found ulterior minds and the cunningness as is found between husbands and wives among you today in their homes. Offensive conduct against spouses and the vile waywardness of children are a nuisance angel. The homes of many believers of today are not in a good state to host angels. Your homes ought to be guest places for holy angels. **I Peter 3:1-7.** Your family lives do not make you deserve to be called the sons and daughters of Sarah. Look! These are the end time days and if someone does not repent, he will perish. **Isaiah 22:12-14.**

21. From the time of old, Satan causes stupid men to not lead their wives with wisdom. Just as Satan

made Sampson sell himself to his wife and brought himself destruction, so are many men of today unable to amend their homes. Look! Victor, listen, it is not Hezekiah alone who has this commandment to repair his home because the end of his life is near but also to you, upon whom the end of the world has come. **Isaiah 38:1-6.** It is for the reason of you changing your evil lifestyles so that the Lord will save you by his mercy that the angel has been sent to proclaim to you the message of salvation for the last. Any one of you, who will listen to these instructions and give them attention and use them to repair his house will have the Lord's salvation. **Psalms 50:22-23.** Victor, take it to them that, the Lord shall in any case give you the type of test he gave his nation in the wilderness, therefore be watchful so that you don't miss target just as they did because Jehovah God by all means tries his people. **Psalms 11:4-5.**

Chapter 2.

Alertness and total trust in God are the assignment of inheritance of the second Adam, uniting him with God through the new covenant.

1. Look! Be alert so that Satan your arch foe does not baffle you. Satan deceived Moses to falter in the wilderness, the reason for which he did not enter the Promised Land. It is the same manner he is jealous against you, to get you strayed like them. Victor, get it clearly that, I, the angel speaking to you I'm the very witness to what happened in the wilderness while I was in the cloud. **Exodus 23:20-26.** While in the cloud, I led the nation with the empowerment of the Most High, and anytime the

nation committed a sin, God power withdrew from their midst. For this reason, any time I moved camp with the nation, I needed to test them to see if they will fend well for the Almighty to guard them. The leading is a promise. **Psalms91:9-12.** What then happened in the wilderness? When the nation strayed and murmured because of thirst, the lord instructed Moses to put some leaf into the Mara river. This is the beginning of their test. **Exodus15:22-27.** After the nation observed that the leaf had healed the water, they re-posted their trust on the leaf as their healing power, not knowing it was a test to them.

2. The lord led them away from the river and brought them to a place of twelve wells for the nation to ask, to whom do the wells and the oil palm trees belong? They should have wanted to know who planted the palm trees and dug the wells. They would have therefore gotten awaken and cast their mind unto Jehovah God alone, for the hope of a man is the Lord. **Jeremiah 17:5-8** The lord led the nation to springing wells to let them know that nothing defeats His arms of creation. The nation never acknowledged it and never their trust perfectly in the Lord. These wells remind God about Abraham. The twelve stands for the family of Jacob, the number according to which Jesus the Lord selected His disciples and the seventy palm trees represent those sent by Christ to proclaim His gospel; standing for the root of Abraham's family in Christ. It was in the sacrifice of atonement made by Christ that the family of Abraham, the father of believers, was chosen.

Gal .3:13-14

3. I know you partake in the body of Christ twelve times a year in accordance with the instruction of Christ's revelation. This puts you in the semblance of Joshua, who also had the sign of twelve. And if you partake in the body of Christ, which is the bread of heaven, then you will by faith receive the blessing of Abraham's family. Look! Take good care of this sign. Amen! The Lord observed that, if the nation remained at the Mara river, which got healed with which got healed with a leaf, they would take it as their healing God. He immediately took them away from there and brought them to the sight of peaceful wells, so that if they are in need, they should ask God for relief.

Psalms 78:12-32 Look! Victor, it is horrifying for one to attempt God. Therefore, you also, be careful today, to not tempt God with lifestyles that stand against His Holy Spirit. **Hebrews 3:7-12** Look! The nation faltered in all the test through which God took them and they never overcome any. Do not be like them.

4. After the Lord led them away from the wells, they were thirsty but instead of calling upon Him, they hardened their hearts and pestered Moses to save them. **Exodus 17:1-7.** Look! It was with much grace that Jehovah protected Moses because, Jethro, his father in-low, who was a stranger rather had trust in God, earlier than the whole of the Israelite nation and even praised the Lord. **Exodus18:7-12.** Look! None of the elders of the Israelite nation ever thought of proclaiming the wonderful things God had done for them. Yet Jethro, who was not an Israelite, and was not even present when they were led out of slavery in Egypt into crossing the red sea rather demonstrated trust in God after Moses had briefed him. God was so much pleased with this act and therefore gave him the wisdom to give Moses good counsel. **Exodus 19:13-24.** As for you, you are strangers, not Israelites, but if you change your minds and worship God according to His orders and precepts, He will demonstrate sufficient kindness in your favours, even more than for Israel. **Psalms 81:12-17**

5. The nation faltered in all the tests given to them by God, due to their hard heartedness and therefore had their skeletons scattered in the wilderness. **Exodus 16:4-5.** You son of man, you will observe according to this scripture that, had the nation reposed their total trust in God, it would not have been their bread alone that would multiply nut the well as well could have been moving with them. **Psalms 23:1-3**. These were the words by which the nation faltered and quested for water, whereas the Lord had promised that He would lead them to fountains. **Psalms1:1-3.** You will notice, according to this scripture that, the nation suffered a lot of want whereas, those led by God normally never suffered want. It was because of this temptation of want that Moses could not enter the promised land, whereas the nation witnessed how the power of God multiplied the manna for them so they will rest assured, yet in spite of all these, they could not have total trust in God. **Exodus 16:25-30.** It is this disobedience in the semblance

of the nation's that is taking place among you today and the abominable things that are abhorrent to God that has filled the hearts of almost everybody. Please, change from such vicious lifestyles. **Hosea 4:1-6.**

6. Listen, Victor, one thing that is essential is for one to realize if God is trying him. The nation did not realize that it was a test being given to them by God, so they were led astray by fear. Moses however realized that is was a trial, so he was not afraid. **Exodus 20:18-20.** The reason many are not being faithful in the worship of God in present day is the fear of death. But as for you, I am getting you awake to be alert and be aware that, most of the temptations you are encountering are trials. The way God tried the forebears and taught them, so does He continue to train people today to learn to rely on Him. Read about the trials of the earlier people in the scripture and use them as examples

to guide yourselves. **Deuteronomy 26:16-19.** People have to overcome their trials and temptations individually before the promises of God get manifest for them. **I Corinthians 10:12-14.** Even after their excessive straying the nation still considered themselves upright in the sight of God. This is the type of deception the devil is using against the children of today, for which many churches have strayed away from everlasting order of the living God. – You need to understand the explanation of the waywardness.

7. This is how it came on the nation: After God decided to save them through the establishment of a covenant, He gave them a commandment through Moses, but they flouted it. Their first ever test, which was thirst took them to the bitter water that could not be drunk, but the Lord healed the water with the leaf of a tree. **Exodus 15:24-27.** This was the instance the nation first saw the miracle of

the leaf and considered it their source of healing power. The Lord quickly corrected them by commanding them to adhere to His covenant, that He, Jehovah is their healer. The nation could not repose their total trust on the Lord but always put their faith on what they saw with their eyes. But as for yon, be aware that those who do not see but believe shall be blessed. **John 20:28-29.** It is imperative that you should be healed of this vicious sickness, so that you would learn to trust in what you have not seen, so that God will treat you as real children. **Hebrews 11:1-2.** Look! That which God never, never approves of is for one to fail to repose his total trust on Him but rather put it on a different thing. This behaviour is very, very distasteful to God. But this is the very behaviour the nation demonstrated towards him in the wilderness.

8. The reward of this vicious lifestyle had been: If ever they will enter my rest! **Psalms 95:6-11.** Proclamation in this Psalm is inviting all of you, not in the manner the nation did it in the wilderness. The nation reposed their trust on wells, so the Lord did not let them find water face to face. In the first instance he led them to a river, except that the water was bitter. He then took them to wells in the second instance, ye they never learned how to repose their trust in Him. This is the reason He did not let them find water, therefore, learn to trust in Him. **Hebrews 2:10-13.** Anyone of you who has the testimony of becoming the son of God through his belief in Jesus should learn how to repose his trust in Him.

9. The nation pestered Moses so much when they felt hungry and failed to rely on their God, who was leading them. When the Lord God however gave them bread, He did not want any to be left over,

because they would have reposed their trust in its availability. **Exodus 16:16-21.** In order to ensure that they did not rely on it, all the remnants melted into fluid under scorching sun. Human beings continue to remain with this behaviour till today. In accordance with the message of the Holy Spirit, if people do not repent, they cannot have salvation. It is in the days of the Holy Spirit you are living today. **Hebrews 3:7-8.** The question is this: what caused the nation to be disobedient? The power of darkness of the queen of heaven caused them to be disobedient to the Lord and He threw them off, for having angered Him, and gave them off to the vicious spirit of the heavenly hosts. **Acts 7:42-45.** The days of David represents the worship order of Jesus, who was raised from the root of David. If you dwell in the days of David and worship God in Jesus, how does your hope on God persist in all your lifestyles?

10. Be careful you do not become the people of the wilderness, for if your trust in God is not complete, you will be left into the worship order of the heavenly hosts. Such people profess the knowledge of God but reject His power. Get ourselves away from them. **Titus 1:16, 2 Timothy 3:5.** God does not want humans to repose their trust in any other creation. Identify this with Him. Amen! The nation pestered Moses again when they felt thirsty, but since God had planned to establish the covenant, He did not consider the nations faltering against Him, but ordered Moses to rally them round and strike the rock. **Exodus 17:4-7.** This rock was not a well. So when the nation came around, they fixed a gaze on Moses and the rock, with the expectation of getting water immediately as it occurred previously. They met a rock, and not a well. This rock stood for the first covenant's laws and its order of worship. It got accomplished that, a sinner must be stoned to death in order to cast the wrong from amongst your midst. Watch the

commandments of the old covenant and you will get this message clear. **(1) Hebrews 12:20-21 (2) Exodus 21:12-17 (3) Leviticus 24:22-23 (4) Leviticus 21:9 (5) Numbers 15:29-31 (6) Numbers 15:32-36.**

11. Consider the fact that the desecration of the day of rest is continuing unabated. If a maiden will tread viciously in her father's household, then you must know that this generation is close to condemnation. **Leviticus 21:9.** The rock of the first covenant was struck, an indication that there is no mercy and grace for those who worship under it. If the Lord were to maintain the covenant of quarrel, then souls would be worn out and the whole nation would perish. **Isaiah 54:7-10, Isaiah 57:15-16.** It is for this reason that God ordered Moses to speak with the rock when the nation felt thirsty once again, but their misbehaviour caused Moses to faulter in the presence of the rock. **Numbers 20:6-12.** Moses

unconsciously struck the rock angry against him, because the second covenant neither lashes nor stones to death. This is the reason Jehovah withdrew Moses' hand and life from the salvation covenant of the second rock. The punishment for this faltering as prescribed by God to Moses was that: Since you did not repose your trust in Me and you did not glorify my name, you will not enter the promised land.

12. It behooves you to be alert so that no one gets unconscious and faulter in the presence of Jehovah your God. Victor, take it to them that, it was to the Mara river that Moses first brought the nation, and later to the wells. These constituted preliminary tests only, but the nation as well as its prophet faltered. The appearance of the rock and its striking represent the might of the old covenant and its commandments. The commandments of the second rock are not like those of the first, and this

represents the new covenant. It is within this that Jesus took a cup and proclaimed about it that: "This is the cup of the everlasting covenant in my blood" **Matthew 26:26-28.** Contemplate this and realized that; had the new covenant brought about mercy and grace, how could humans be saved? What does the scripture say? The rock that followed them was Christ.

13. Know it then that, the sin which is not forgiven in Moses within the commandments of the old covenant are forgiven in Christ in accordance with the commandments of the new covenant. **Hebrews 9:15.** Christ the custodian of the new covenant and it is within him that atonement and the payment of debts are perfectly obtained. **Hebrews 7:22-25.** It is imperative to abrogate the old covenant because it was full of wickedness and curse. **Hebrews 7:18-19.** The law does not make anyone perfect, the reason for which we are brought the covenant that will

help us get more closer to God that before which is the covenant in the blood of the Lord Jesus Christ. Now then, Jesus has committed the leadership of the church into the hands of the Holy Spirit. The devil is however confusing people in matters of the order of worship. I will therefore explain to you the methods he applies for the confusion so that you will hear all and remain alert.

14. Jesus the Lord knows it that, it is only the efforts of the Holy Spirit that can build the Lord's church in order that humans have eternal life. If the Holy Spirit does not testify and confirm the sonship of a person, one cannot enter the heavenly kingdom. This is the reason the Lord declared that, without the coming of the Comforter, there shall be no respite. **John 16:5-7.** Without the coming of the Holy Spirit, one cannot be born to go to heaven. Jesus the Lord gave the Jewish teachers a confirmation of this **John 3:3-12.** It is the

responsibility of the Holy Spirit to witness about the baptism of a person. Just as the Father and the Son exist from the very beginning, so does exist the order of baptism. The Holy Spirit must receive witnessing from the Father about a person and again receive it from the Son to the effect that the person believes in the Son. Thereafter, the Spirit Himself will give confirmation with His own witnessing, to the witnessing of the earlier two in order to confirm the witnessing the three.

15. If the Spirit does not receive a witnessing from the Father and the Son, the Spirit cannot offer His witnessing, meanwhile, it is His primary responsibility to confirm the witnessing. **I. John 5:6-8.** This witnessing conforms with the eternal life commandment of the Lord, as the life-giving order that; one person should not testify against a sinner that deserves to die. So did it occur that when Adam committed the sin that deserved death he

inherited death in accordance with the word of witnesses. **Deuteronomy 19:15, & 17:6.** Humans inherited sin from the first Adam and it brought about death. In order not to kill one who inherited sin in the era of Christ, there is the need for three witnesses to confirm the reason why the person should not die. Humans inherited sin and death in the first Adam. We however inherit eternal life in the Second Adam through our belief in Christ because this Second Adam comes from heaven and knows no sin, the reason for which He is a Victor. **John 8:23-24.**

16. The Second Adam is from heaven and He is the spirit which gives life. **I. Corinthians 15:45-49.** It is because of God's desire that humans possess the nature of the Second Adam that He sent the Son to the world, and after the Son accomplished his mission, He put the church under the power of the Holy Spirit. This is the reason it is said that; if you

hear the voice of the spirit today, do not harden your hearts. **Hebrews 3:7-8** Jesus the Lord indicated that, when the Holy Spirit comes, He shall teach you and lead you into the whole perfect truth. This confirms that, Christ appointed the Holy Spirit as the teacher of the church. **John 16:12-15.** The signs of today's hardheartedness are already demonstrated in the church. But as for you, ensure that this hardheartedness does not persist in the church. If the Lord's appointed teacher for the church is rejected, but schools have been established for their priests to go and learn, then it means that these schools have become institutions of default against the doctrines of God. Observe the first people! After they received the Holy Spirit as their teacher, they engaged in serious prayers and fasting until the Spirit Himself appointed those to be sent on mission. **Acts 13:1-3.**

17. Teach yourselves with the examples of the people mentioned in the scriptures, so that the Spirit Himself would choose your leaders for you. The people of today select their choice of priest to their schools and believe that they can apply secular knowledge to the understanding of spiritual things. This amounts to a default in the understanding of the Holy Spirit because the understanding remains that it is with the Holy Spirit that spiritual things are understood and not secular knowledge. **I Corinthians 2:10-14.** It is the spirit of the world that incites the churches with disobedience; pray fervently therefore that this spirit does not deceive you. It is the sign of disobedience to apply wrong methods in the mission of the spirit or submit the mission unto the authority of humans. This action is very vicious in the eyes of Jehovah God. It is the duty of the Holy Spirit to lead those who deserve salvation into the church. **Acts 2:38-41.** The sign of disobedience that goes along with leading souls into the church is

how the spirit of the world is drawing souls unto himself with the want of food and clothing. The message of the kingdom of heaven however has nothing to do with food and drinks. **Romans 14:17-20.**

18. It remains in the understanding of the Holy Spirit that the gospel be proclaimed for humans to repent and become firm believers. **Romans 10:16-17.** If humans would not be affirmed with the life-giving gospel but would rather be wooed with food, clothing and the supply of needs, then the person's path of salvation is completely destroyed. As for you, strive to lay a sound foundation for the people in the church with the true gospel, so that you will accomplish the sealing of the covenant of Christ Jesus for the receipt of eternal life for yourself as well as the church. This will ensure amidst you, the perfection of the love of our Lord Jesus Christ and

God, the Father, and the signs of the fellowship of the Holy Spirit. **2 Corinthians 13:13.**

19.   Another sign of disobedience ruling in the present era is the use of the weaknesses of the apostles as a weapon to destroy the orders of the Holy Spirit. Look! The Lord Jesus instructed His disciples to baptize people in the power of the three witnesses. **Matthew 28:18-20.** The people of today have altered this word and have come to replace it with Peter's explanation of an issue related to repentance, and have held onto that to baptize people in the name of Jesus. This is the spirit of misunderstanding ruling the world. Be careful about this spirit. **Acts 2:38.** The apostle was only explaining an issue and it was not what he was referring to at that time that people are practicing today.   Another   sign   of   hardheartedness   is committing the church unto the worship of ulterior spirits, claiming it to be the Holy Spirit. Look! The

order is that; "He shall take from mine and will not speak on His own". **John 16:14.**

20. Anything that Jesus did not do but people have courage to do same in Christian churches amounts to abandoning the Holy Spirit and following other spirits. For instance, from whose are lighting candles and incense, the use of oils and holy water deduced? Look! Victor, be very much alert. The order of breaking of bread from house to house by the apostles was received through a vision by Paul from the Lord Jesus Christ and he testified thus: "But I, what I received from the Lord is what I gave to you". **I Corinthians 11:23-25.** These and a lot more did the Lord correct through Paul and he indicated that, when I come, I will correct all what remain. **I. Corinthians 11:33-34.** The Lord Jesus Himself had accomplished what was to be corrected and He revealed it through a prophecy that: "the bread of life is the one that descended

from heaven which bears twelve fruits each month; which signifies the commandment establishing the holy communion; for, it has a programmed period of celebration since the time of the old covenant. So does it also have its time of celebration in the time of the new covenant, to be observed accordingly. **Numbers 9:13.**

21. Observe the orders practiced by Christ, so you will not become hardhearted in the affairs of the Holy Spirit. **Revelation 22:1-2.** Take care you do not alter the understanding of these issues. Anybody who alters the understanding of the scripture or turns it upside down draws upon himself his own destruction. **II. Peter 3:14-16.** You will observe from these alterations that the Holy Spirit Himself taught Paul that tongue speaking was needless in the church. He himself testified, he would rather pray in five intelligible words rather than speak ten thousand words in tongues. The

children of today have rather altered this to mean that tongues signify the baptism of the Holy Spirit – this amounts to straying from the spirit of the truth. If you clearly understand what Paul meant; you will not stray off. **I. Corinthians 14:16-22.** What the Holy Spirit taught Paul, according to God's commandment is that, tongues are not a sign for believers. The children of today have altered this for themselves, to the extent that that which does not belong to believers is what they have chosen for themselves – their plight is very pathetic. The spirit of the world has cuffed them and has enburdened them with this strange order, thus rendering their hope for the promises void.

22. The reason their hope is dashed is that, they are not able to understand the Holy Spirit. Look! The Holy Spirit taught Paul that, that which is halved, does not abide within the whole, because halves are only halves and they ought to be

discarded to give place to the establishment of the perfection, for it is within this that the promise of eternal life abides. **Matthew 5:48.** Halves are of no value in the lifestyles of a believer. **I. Corinthians 13:8-10.** Even in these instances, the spirit of the world has altered their understanding to consider the signs of halves as a mark of spiritual progress in the sight of God. The fact remains that tongues neither constitute any growth in Christ nor an advancement in God in way. The perfect growth is the progress in the love and the power by which one will be able to overcome temptation. II Peter3:17-18, Eph.4:11-16 Look! Victor, if any of you will consider these as mere pronouncements from humans and have no need for them, then he deceives himself for you have been ordained as a prophet and a teacher, who should apply perfect knowledge to teach for progress of the generations of today into eternal life.

CHAPTER 3

The serpent is the agent of enmity separation the children of the lamb and the offspring of the beast. The bearers of the mark of the beast are already in judgment.

1. You are therefore hearing my voice from the holy of holies, where Jesus himself constitutes the foundation; so, give perfect attention to these messages. **Hebrews 6:19-20.** Today's generation does no longer adhere to order of healing instituted by God for believers. **Jam. 5:14-16.** They falter in this scripture and many churches have resorted to the harvest of herbs, claiming the possess healing power. Some churches have adopted the application of various drugs and others cast out demons by tying up people and torturing them. The question for such people is

that, from whose order should their practices be deduced? These are deception ways of the world. As for you; I beseech you to tread the path of the Lord Jesus Christ, for he has left an example for you to follow, so you do not harden your hearts against the spirit of the Lord. **I. Peter 2:21.** Everybody is going to give account to Jehovah God about all that he did in this life, but woe unto those who will not take from the order of the Lord Jesus. For this reason, be alert in your souls for the Lord is near.

2. A dangerous weapon being applied by Satan to incite disobedience in Christian churches of today is the use of beautiful women and smart ladies. They are unable to abide by rulers and yet, no one withdraws them from the church, for the reason that, there exist secrets between them and leader and the frontliners of the churches. Satan is able to get attractive ladies into the church from under sea world, who use their beauty to desecrate the church. The queen of heaven also sends ladies from the skies or from large rivers into the churches.

They are serpents, not born by humans, but are extremely beautiful that, it becomes difficult for me to escape their whims. They befriend ladies born of humans and teach them how to desecrate God. They teach them how to sell their beauty at exorbitant rates and how to apply high lifestyles and excessive adornments as well as pride and jealousy to make the saints of the church fall off their faith unconsciously.

3. When the priests are caught with their charms, they lie to the church, claiming the spirit has chosen the ladies for special assignments in the promotion of the gospel. Some are ordained as prophets for their churches and all their prophecies linger on the search for worldly needs. Some even strive to become leaders, who then institute nothing but lies in the Holy Spirit. They, with their charms draw the unfirm to themselves to be deceived and cheated. **Ezekiel 13:17-19.** The spirit of the world has made the churches of today to prefer lies and deception to the hearing of the

perfect truth. The activities of these lady-captives of the spirit have made corruption the ruling fashion in almost all the churches, for they, by their charms sender unfirm men captives. **2 Timothy 3:5-8.** The power of such spirit altar the minds of many people to stand against the truth.

4. They hate those who possess the truth and their churches betray those who abide in truth into destruction. Looks Victor, you need alertness and serious prayers, for these are signs of the end time. **I Peter 4:7-8.** Since it is a conspiracy by Satan, he will not declare the instances in which to get them trapped, but if you keep alert through prayers, you will overcome him. The Holy Spirit of God did not write his messages. All that the Lord Jesus said about it is that. If he comes, he shall load you into the remaining issues. In this case also, it is only through prayers that you will understand them. You need to be alert in adhering to all these, as the only way by which you will overcome the cunning ways of the Spirit of the world. If you however miss

the path of the Holy Spirit, you will forever perish. Look, it is the Spirit which quickens, the flesh profits nothing and it is in eternal life. **Ephesians. 4: 30.**

5. You will notice that, the Spirit testifies with your own Spirit that you are the sons of God. For this reason, do not flout the teachings of Holy Spirit. If you flout the teachings of Holy Spirit, which covenant will God apply to save you into life? You know the first covenant was one of wickedness, the reason, for which the rock was struck with a stick. The commandment given to Moses was that, set a limit for the nation and if any one goes beyond the limit, he shall die. **Exodus 19:21-25.** The commandment given by the new covenant is to speak to the hearing of the nation, for them to obey because, there is no limit set between God and those heart the commandment written. **Hebrews 10:15-17.** All things must be under the control of Holy Spirit so that there would not be any limit or the wall of strife between you and

heaven. If the church is taken away from the Holy Spirit and put under the weakness of the apostles, then there shall be a limit between the church and heaven. Most of the activities of the apostles have weaknesses in them. So, you must be alert against them.

6. For instance, some of apostles baptized people, but not according to what proceeded out of the mouth of Jesus. Jesus the Lord instructed that baptism must be done in the name of God, the Father, God, the Son and God the Holy Spirit. Some of Christ's disciples said, baptism should be done in the name of Jesus. **Acts. 8:14-17.** No limits exist between a church which is under the leadership of the Holy Spirit and the Spirit Himself. This enables enable the Holy Spirit to lead those who deserve eternal life into the church. The Spirit Himself heals the church of its ailments, this enabling the content of the Psalm to work in the church. **Psalms 103:1-5.** This scripture encourages believers to remain stead fact and overcome the afflictions that will come in

the end time. **Hebrews 10:15-17.** Look! The limits of the old covenant draw along anger and death but the adherence to the lows of Holy Spirit removes the wall of separation which is the limit and therefore shall be blessed all who will remove the wall of strife though their obedience to the Holy Spirit. **Colossians 1:19-23.**

7. Take note that, the ruling power of drug over faith, churches are from the fight of the beast. They shall be blessed, those who overcome the beast and its idol. **Revelation 11:18-19.** The Holy Spirit must heal the prayers of the members of the church so that they will be able to offer healing to the ailments of all members. Fools claim that God heals spiritual ailments only, so carnal knowledge should be used to heal physical ailments. The question is that, human flesh is like God who created all flesh, and would therefore heal the ailment which Jehovah God can not heal? There is nothing ever beyond the power of God almighty. **Jeremiah 32:27, Jeremiah 27:5.** Jehovah God, after

creating the whole body; will he be unable to heal a part of him?

8. Look! The beast knows God's plans time of Eden that, it is from the blessing of glory that grows the roots of the trees in the garden, so does the use of tree possess the power of healing. **Genesis 2:16-17.** This is the reason man never know any ailments while living in the garden and feeding on the fruits of the trees. God instructed him not to eat the fruit of the tree that brings curse and death. Since Satan wanted a strife between God and man, he beguiled the woman and the husband and they ate of the fruit of the tree curse and death and therefore flouted the low of life. Then Jehovah God immediately convened a meeting on the mount of congregation to deliberated on what to do for man. In this council of the meeting, the sought counsel as to which punishment to mete out the man to suit his sin. The counsel indicated that, man be driven out of the garden of life and peace. **Genesis 3:22-24.** Now Victor, let me unveil your mind to

clear your spiritual eyes so that the cover put on the mind of the humans by the beast will be taken off your mind so that you will clearly understand the scriptures. Think of the counsel of heaven and be aware that, it was then that it was decreed that, man should not stretch his hands and pluck the fruit of the tree of live for consumption, so that he will live endlessly. Man, therefore drawn away from the tree of life.

9. It then became a law in heaven that, man must never on his own pluck the fruit of the tree of life for consumption. The beast however has incited the inhabitants of the earth to harvest the roots of the trees for use as drug to provide life. This ideal stands against the rules and counsel of heaven. Therefore, all people, who are groping in search of life are considered iniquitous under the lows of the counsel's fellowship. Do not do such a thing so that you will not get into the grips of the conviction of these counselors. **Matthew 5:21-22.** These counselors are great cherubs who have been

commanded the God Almighty to ensure that humans do not on their own stretch their hands and pluck the life provider for themselves. Therefore, those who are groping in search of life for them-selves have by this action already declared themselves guilty. The beast is out with every effort that all Christian churches should fall into this guilt. Blest be all those who repose their trust in the Lord Almighty, for they are the shareholders in the heavenly call. **Hebrews 2:10-13**

10. I am advising you, who are shareholders in the heavenly fellowship call that you not let these great heavenly counselors see you to stretching your hands in search of life for yourselves. Behold, it was only one commandment given to man about the tree of life in the garden of Eden. It is this, that; the you shall stretch your hand and pluck the fruit of the knowledge of right and wrong you shall die. After man had fallen into sin, the heavenly council, whose head and chair is Christ Jesus himself, it was decreed that, man should never attempt for

harvest the fruits of the tree of live. The force of low is that, even if the tree is openly exposed, you, yourself, do not touch it your own. Blessed are those who are able to overcome in the sight of these counselors. The strife increases between God and Humans, if people think they can obtain life through the application of regimen, for the purpose for which cherub are guarding the tree of life is to ensure that, humans do not touch it. If you however attempt it, then it means, you want to devise some means to touch it, and when you are caught by the cherubs. You shall fall into their wrath disrupting their charge. This because you have applied a cunning measure at the time they were in total alertness with the tree of life. If human securities are guarding something and you pass behind them to steal some of it and you are caught, low will they treat you?

11. The cherubs will always protect you, while in their charge of watch over the tree of life, they notice that, you belong to the fellowship of those

who do not touch the tree of life on your own. They will be pleased with you, if they find you to be obedient children who are not persecutors of the tree of life. Then will they become errand runners for your church. **Psalms 91:9-13.** The psalm contains the power with which the cherubs work in the church and this ought to manifest for the church as had been written. Look! Do not let yourselves be found guilty by these great heavenly counselors. The stripes of Jesus must work on all who have been cleansed of their sins, so that they will receive the mask which enables the cherubs to take good care of you. I Peter2:24-25. This scripture proves that, if one has the sign of the lamb, he is identified by the cherubs as a partaker in the tree of life. It is upon the power of this sign that cherubs open the doors to the tree for one to come to it all the time. **Revelation 22:13-14.**

12. Fools claim that, it is God who created the herbs and trees to be used healing. Contemplate about this, if God had created something for the

healing of humans, why then should He charge guards to watch the tree; which is to heal? Be aware that, it is not for reason of beasts destroying its fruits that Jehovah God has charged angels to guard the gates. The purpose of the watch rather is that, humans should not touch the tree, let alone eat of its fruits, so they do not live forever with evil nature. Do you think that, the cherubs will guard the tree of life, without guarding the herbs and the trees? That would be stupid from the day Jehovah God cursed the earth because of humans, the whole earth and all its offspring got engulfed the cursed. Behold! It is known to the great heavenly counselors that; God has permitted humans to pray and get out of the grips of the curse. **Jam. 5:1-16.** If one does not apply the prayer method, but some other method, he has strayed and will be defeated by the beast because of his unbelief

13. The beast is seriously at work with the enmity which God has established between the serpent and the offspring of humans in these last days.

Genesis 3:15. The beast has come to place this enmity between humans and Jesus Christ. The beast, Laving observed that God has cursed the earth and all its up springs, has come to establish its mark on drugs. There is nothing Christ to be applied by the beast to put the mark of its idol on humans, so has he incited Christians to approve drug as the healing power and by so doing, the beast is encouraged to mark all believer-drug-captives with his sign. They consider themselves Christians but rather belong to the beast completely. Probe into this example and know it that Jehovah God does not change. **Numbers 21:7-9, Isaiah 41:4.** Jehovah God, knowing that, the trees and the herbs are curses, did not allow Moses to heal anybody which any of these things. He instructed them to look on the bronze image of the snake and those who were stricken by vermin of the snake bite got healed by their sight of the snake. God continues to deliver people through his Son Jesus Christ, who went on the cross. Just as

Moses did not anybody to use any other means to stop the venom of the snake, so does the Son of Man, who went on the cross also not permit anybody to apply any other means to stop the pangs of ailments.

14. The commandment is that, humans should fix gaze on the Son of Man with faith and remain alive. **John 3:14-15, II Chronicles 16:12-15, Isaiah 38:1-7, Isaiah 7:10-14, Isaiah 53:5.** Since the snake fabricated by Moses in the wilderness was of bronze, it could not baffle people but the serpent which beguiled Ever is in Spirit baffling people today. **2 Corinthians 11:3.** The primary means applied by the serpent to plant enmity between Christ and humans is drug healing. Other includes wrong marriage and advanced liberal lifestyles which the teachings of Christ prohibit. If you are believer in God, who loves Christ, yet your spirit stands against faith healing with the stripes of Christ by prayer a mere trifle then you must know that the beast has captured you and you are a

captive to its sign. The beast desires that all humans in the world remain under the curse through drug healing. So that the kingdom of the beast will rule the earth in place of that of the Lamb of God. By so doing, a bitter enmity will remain between believers who have the mark of the beast and believers who deny drug healing so the former will fight for the beast. **Colossians 1:19-23.**

15. The beast incites those conquered by him with the fear of death and has captured their minds to believe that, if something does not contain drug, then it is not complete. For instance, it is always intended that, drug be, by all means applied to a believer woman who delivers a child before a sick person, the children of the beast would by all means want the healing to be confirmed by the application of some drug. Satan knows that medication is an idol worship on its own, the reason for which he causes people to be compelled into drug application as a sign of loving life and its

defense; so that, if some people should deny it, then the state authorities will arrest them, try them and commit them to prison. Believes who have the mark of the beast hold onto the understanding that, medication is the arm of deliverance of God.

16. The beast has imbibed it in those conquered by him to repose all their trust in medication. Look! Victor, the time has come for all who deny medication to be persecuted, just as Jesus the Lord was persecuted, so that what Jesus prophesied be manifest in you. **John 15:18-27.** This phase, which says I am the one they first hate, implies that, believers should be alert, before one expresses hatred or blasphemy against you, such a one should first of all denigrate your faith, which is in Christ. But as for you, pronounce no word against them. Furthermore, do not allow yourselves to get involved in matters of money, plots of land, the inheritance of homes as well as other frivolous matters that will invite their hatred against you, so that they do not blaspheme your faith. All those

who have overcome the beast and its mark hold onto this understanding that it is Jehovah God, who caused all the content of the scripture to be written from within his own spirit.

II Peter 1:19-21.

17. Look! The only thing which is able to conquer the beast and its mark is living according to that which has been written from within God's spirit. The beast gets wild against people who live according to the scripture proceeding from the spirit of God, for he is aware that, their faith, which is built on the scripture, has already conquered the world. Before somebody's faith is able to conquer the world, he ought to build it on the scriptures proceeding from the spirit of God. It is a must that your faith should conquer the world. **I John 5:2-5.** It must be clear to you, Victor, that the beast will seriously prosecute chosen believers in these last days, compelling believers to put more trust in medication than in faithful prayers. It well even

come to pass that believers will find more contentment in medication than reposing their trust in prayers. This will cause a cessation to the existence of faithful prayer supplicants amongst you on earth. The beast will institute cunning means to make people consider the faith as mere prayers. The faith supersedes all is the glorious one, on which one should build himself for eternal life.

18. Look! Frightening days are coming end laws are going to be forceful and life is going to be difficult for believers who do not ascribe to medication. They themselves and their children will be exposed to public ridicule, denigration and jeering because of the faith. **Hebrews 10:32-33.** To the serpent belong drug and he is father to his own and it applies the power of its mark in war against the Lamb. To the Lamb also belong his blood and stripes. All believers who will stand for his blood and his stripes will suffer and shall be tortured in the presence of believer-drug-captives. Some will be spied on and be betrayed. People who do not

have the sign of drug and medical certification will find it very difficult in those days to have employment and trading will be restricted.

19. It will come to pass that, those who do not ascribe to medication will be charged for spreading diseases among the populace. There shall come a time, when there will be no church which will believe in the stripes of Christ, because their arms shall go down. **Daniel 11:32-37.** I have told you all these for your steadfastness. May you be guided on by the spirit of patience and long suffering of our Lord Jesus Christ. **Hebrews 13:20-21.** Amen.

Printed in Great Britain
by Amazon